Spanish Language Lessons

Level 1 Beginners Guide To Learning And Speaking The Spanish Language
(1000 Most Popular Words, Basic Conversation, Spain Travel Guide & Short Stories)

Love New Languages

© Copyright 2018 - All rights reserved.

It is not legal to reproduce, duplicate, or transmit any part of this document in either electronic means or in printed format. Recording of this publication is strictly prohibited and any storage of this document is not allowed unless with written permission from the publisher except for the use of brief quotations in a book review.

Table of Contents

Introduction 4
Chapter 1: Basic Conversation 5
Chapter 2: Days, Months and Weather 16
Chapter 3: Numbers 1-100 and Ordinal Numbers 17
Chapter 4: Places and Animals 21
Chapter 5: Description, Clothes, Colors and Body Parts 25
Chapter 6: Food, Fruits and Vegetables 28
Chapter 7: Family and People 30
Chapter 8: Feelings and Emotions 31
Chapter 9: Sports and Activities 32
Chapter 10: Professions 33
Chapter 11: Countries and Nationalities 34
Chapter 12: Cognates 37
Chapter 13: 1000 Most Used Words 51
Chapter 14: One Word, Several Meanings. 79
Chapter 15: Small Real Life Stories 107
Conclusion 119

Introduction

Welcome to Spanish Language Lessons. Get excited because you're about to learn how to speak Spanish as a beginner. More and more people are dedicating their time to learn a language because it improves your communicative skills, and offers you more opportunities in life, especially when traveling. Some people still believe that you need to have a lot of time to do it or you need to be very smart. The truth is that because this book is an audiobook you can constantly listen and learn, and even multi task it. Cleaning the house, driving home from work, or on the train? Cool, plug in to this audiobook and keep listening. You will notice a gradual increase in your capabilities while you killed 2 birds with one stone. Learning the language soley depends on you, the enthusiasm and the interest you put to it. There are many ways to learn a language and many methods to use. You just have to find the one that works better for you.

This audiobook is made for a beginner audience with no difference of age and is perfect for those who prefer listening than reading. Of course, it does not include every word you need to know in Spanish, but it has enough words for you to have a very strong base. The audiobook contains: Basic conversation, days, months, weather; numbers; animals; places, rooms, clothes, colors, body parts; food, vegetables, family, people; feelings, emotions, sports, activities; professions; countries and nationalities. The chapters twelve to fifteen have subjects a little different such as cognates, the thousand most used words, one-word several meanings, and small real-life stories which are sentences for you to practice comprehension and vocabulary.

Remember, this is a guide for your learning process, but you can have your own way to use it. You are free to listen and repeat as many times as you need. Let's start now!

Chapter 1: Basic Conversation

Words:

1)

Hello means Hola

Now say it yourself: Hola

Great! **Hello means** Hola

2)

Hi, My Name is means Hola, mi nombre es

Now say it yourself: Hola, mi nombre es... John

Great! **My Name is means** Hola, mi nombre es

3)

How are you means ¿Cómo estás?

Now say it yourself: ¿Cómo estás?

Great! **How are you means** ¿Cómo estás?

4)

Nice to meet you means Mucho gusto

Now say it yourself: Mucho gusto

Great! **Nice to meet you means** Mucho gusto

5)

Good, what about you means Bien, ¿y tú?

Now say it yourself: Bien, ¿y tú?

Great! **Good, what about you means** Bien, ¿y tú?

6)

What's the time? means ¿Qué hora es?

Now say it yourself: ¿Qué hora es?

Great! **What's the time? means** ¿Qué hora es?

7)

Where is? means ¿Dónde está...?

Now say it yourself: ¿Dónde está...?

Great! **Where is? means** ¿Dónde está...?

8)

How was your weekend means ¿Qué tal tu fin de semana?

Now say it yourself: ¿Qué tal tu fin de semana?

Great! **How was your weekend means** ¿Qué tal tu fin de semana?

9)

How has your day been? means ¿Qué tal tu día?

Now say it yourself: ¿Qué tal tu día?

Great! **How has your day been? means** ¿Qué tal tu día?

10)

Where are you from? **means** ¿De dónde eres?

Now say it yourself: ¿De dónde eres?

Great! Where are you from? **means** ¿De dónde eres?

11)

What's your number? **means** ¿Cuál es tu número de teléfono?

Now say it yourself: ¿Cuál es tu número de teléfono?

Great! What's your number? **means** ¿Cuál es tu número de teléfono?

12)

You look good today **means** ¡Te ves bien!

Now say it yourself: ¡Te ves bien!

Great! You look good today **means** ¡Te ves bien!

13)

Where is the closest restaurant? **means** ¿Dónde queda el restaurant más cercano?

Now say it yourself: ¿Dónde queda el restaurant más cercano?

Great! Where is the closest restaurant? **means** ¿Dónde queda el restaurant más cercano?

14)

What do you do for fun? means ¿Qué te gusta hacer?

Now say it yourself: ¿Qué te gusta hacer?

Great! **What do you do for fun? means** ¿Qué te gusta hacer?

15)

What's your job? means ¿Cuál es tu trabajo?

Now say it yourself: ¿Cuál es tu trabajo?

Great! **What's your job? means** ¿Cuál es tu trabajo?

16)

Where do you work? means ¿Dónde trabajas?

Now say it yourself: ¿Dónde trabajas?

Great! **Where do you work? means** ¿Dónde trabajas?

17)

I need help means Necesito ayuda

Now say it yourself: Necesito ayuda

Great! **I need help means** Necesito ayuda

18)

Take care, see you! means ¡Cuídate! Nos vemos

Now say it yourself: ¡Cuídate! Nos vemos

Great! **Take care, see you! means** ¡Cuídate! Nos vemos

19)

Goodbye means Adiós

Now say it yourself: Adiós

Great! **Goodbye means** Adiós

20)

Please means Por favor

Now say it yourself: Por favor

Great! **Please means** Por favor

21)

Thanks/ Thank you means Gracias

Now say it yourself: Gracias

Great! **Thanks/ Thank you means** Gracias

22)

Thank you very much means Muchas gracias

Now say it yourself: Muchas gracias

Great! **Thank you very much means** Muchas gracias

23)

You're welcome means De nada

Now say it yourself: De nada

Great! **You're welcome means** De nada

24)

I'm sorry means Lo siento

Now say it yourself: Lo siento

Great! **I'm sorry means** Lo siento

25)

Excuse me means Permiso

Now say it yourself: Permiso

Great! **Excuse me means** Permiso

26)

Good morning means Buenos días

Now say it yourself: Buenos días

Great! **Good morning means** Buenos días

27)

Good night means Buenas noches

Now say it yourself: Buenas noches

Great! **Good night means** Buenas noches

28)

Good afternoon/ evening means Buenas tardes

Now say it yourself: Buenas tardes

Great! **Good afternoon/ evening means** Buenas tardes

29)

See you soon **means** Nos vemos pronto

Now say it yourself: Nos vemos pronto

Great! See you soon **means** Nos vemos pronto

30)

See you later **means** Nos vemos luego

Now say it yourself: Nos vemos luego

Great! See you later **means** Nos vemos luego

31)

See you tomorrow **means** Nos vemos mañana

Now say it yourself: Nos vemos mañana

Great! See you tomorrow **means** Nos vemos mañana

32)

Have a nice day **means** ¡Que tengas buen día!

Now say it yourself: ¡Que tengas buen día!

Great! Have a nice day **means** ¡Que tengas buen día!

33)

What date is today? **means** ¿Qué fecha es hoy?

Now say it yourself: ¿Qué fecha es hoy?

Great! What date is today? **means** ¿Qué fecha es hoy?

34)

What's your last name/ surname? **means** ¿Cuál es tu apellido?

Now say it yourself: ¿Cuál es tu apellido?

Great! What's your last name/ surname? **means** ¿Cuál es tu apellido?

35)

Do you have a nickname? **means** ¿Tienes un apodo?

Now say it yourself: ¿Tienes un apodo?

Great! Do you have a nickname? **means** ¿Tienes un apodo?

36)

What do you do? **means** ¿A qué te dedicas?

Now say it yourself: ¿A qué te dedicas?

Great! What do you do? **means** ¿A qué te dedicas?

37)

What are you doing? **means** ¿Qué haces?

Now say it yourself: ¿Qué haces?

Great! What are you doing? **means** ¿Qué haces?

38)

Are you ok? **means** ¿Estás bien?

Now say it yourself: ¿Estás bien?

Great! Are you ok? **means** ¿Estás bien?

39)

How do you feel? means ¿Cómo te sientes?

Now say it yourself: ¿Cómo te sientes?

Great! **How do you feel? means** ¿Cómo te sientes?

40)

Where do you live? means ¿Dónde vives?

Now say it yourself: ¿Dónde vives?

Great! **Where do you live? means** ¿Dónde vives?

41)

Could you please help me? means ¿Podrías ayudarme, por favor?

Now say it yourself: ¿Podrías ayudarme, por favor?

Great! **Could you please help me? means** ¿Podrías ayudarme, por favor?

42)

May I help you? means ¿Puedo ayudarte?

Now say it yourself: ¿Puedo ayudarte?

Great! **May I help you? means** ¿Puedo ayudarte?

43)

Do you speak English/Spanish? means ¿Hablas inglés/ español?

Now say it yourself: ¿Hablas inglés/ español?

Great! **Do you speak English/Spanish? means** ¿Hablas inglés/ español?

44)

How old are you? **means** ¿Qué edad tienes?

Now say it yourself: ¿Qué edad tienes?

Great! How old are you? **means** ¿Qué edad tienes?

45)

When is your birthday? **means** ¿Cuándo es tu cumpleaños?

Now say it yourself: ¿Cuándo es tu cumpleaños?

Great! When is your birthday? **means** ¿Cuándo es tu cumpleaños?

46)

Do you like movies or TV series? **means** ¿Te gustan las películas o las series de television?

Now say it yourself: ¿Te gustan las películas o las series de television?

Great! Do you like movies or TV series? **means** ¿Te gustan las películas o las series de television?

47)

Where do you study? **means** ¿Dónde estudias?

Now say it yourself: ¿Dónde estudias?

Great! Where do you study? **means** ¿Dónde estudias?

48)

Would you please repeat? means ¿Puedes repetir, por favor?

Now say it yourself: ¿Puedes repetir, por favor?

Great! **Would you please repeat? means** ¿Puedes repetir, por favor?

49)

What does that mean? means ¿Qué significa...?

Now say it yourself: ¿Qué significa...?

Great! **What does that mean? means** ¿Qué significa...?

50)

How do you say... means ¿Cómo se dice...?

Now say it yourself: ¿Cómo se dice...?

Great! **How do you say... means** ¿Cómo se dice...?

51)

May I borrow your...? means ¿Podrías prestarme tu...?

Now say it yourself: ¿Podrías prestarme tu...?

Great! **May I borrow your...? means** ¿Podrías prestarme tu...?

Chapter 2: Days, Months and Weather

Days of the week

Monday is Lunes
Tuesday is Martes
Wednesday is Miércoles
Thursday is Jueves
Friday is Viernes
Saturday is Sábado
Sunday is Domingo

Months

January is Enero
February is Febrero
March is Marzo
April is Abril
May is Mayo
June is Junio
July is Julio
August is Agosto
September is Septiembre
October is Octubre
November is Noviembre
December is Diciembre

Weather and Times of the Day

Autumn is otoño
Cloudy is nublado
Cold is frío
Day is día
Evening is tarde
Fog is neblina
Freeze is helada
Fresh is fresco
Hot is caliente
Lightning is relámpago
Midday is mediodía
Midnight is medianoche
Moon is luna
Morning is mañana
Night is noche
Rain is lluvia
Rainy is lluvioso
Season is estación
Snow is nieve
Spring is primavera
Star is estrella
Storm is tormenta
Summer is verano
Sun is sol
Sunny is soleado
Sunrise is amanecer
Sunset is atardecer
Thunder is trueno
Tropical is tropical
Warmth is calor
Wind is viento
Winter is invierno

Chapter 3: Numbers 1-100 and Ordinal Numbers

Numbers 1-100

0. zero in Spanish is cero
1. one is uno
2. two is dos
3. three is tres
4. four is cuatro
5. five is cinco
6. six is seis
7. seven is siete
8. eight is ocho
9. nine is nueve
10. ten is diez
11. eleven is once
12. twelve is doce
13. thirteen is trece
14. fourteen is catorce
15. fifteen is quince
16. sixteen is dieciséis
17. seventeen is diecisiete
18. eighteen is dieciocho
19. nineteen is diecinueve
20. twenty is veinte
21. twenty-one is veintiuno
22. twenty-two is veintidós
23. twenty-three is veintitrés
24. twenty-four is veinticuatro
25. twenty-five is veinticinco
26. twenty-six is veintiséis
27. twenty-seven is veintisiete
28. twenty-eight is veintiocho
29. twenty-nine is veintinueve
30. thirty is treinta
31. thirty-one is treinta y uno

32. thirty-two is treinta y dos
33. thirty-three is treinta y tres
34. thirty-four is treinta y cuatro
35. thirty-five is treinta y cinco
36. thirty-six is treinta y seis
37. thirty-seven is treinta y siete
38. thirty-eight is treinta y ocho
39. thirty-nine is treinta y nueve
40. forty is cuarenta
41. forty-one is cuarenta y uno
42. forty-two is cuarenta y dos
43. forty-three is cuarenta y tres
44. forty-four is cuarenta y cuatro
45. forty-five is cuarenta y cinco
46. forty-six is cuarenta y seis
47. forty-seven is cuarenta y siete
48. forty-eight is cuarenta y ocho
49. forty-nine is cuarenta y nueve
50. fifty is cincuenta
51. fifty-one is cincuenta y uno
52. fifty-two is cincuenta y dos
53. fifty-three is cincuenta y tres
54. fifty-four is cincuenta y cuatro
55. fifty-five is cincuenta y cinco
56. fifty-six is cincuenta y seis
57. fifty-seven is cincuenta y siete
58. fifty-eight is cincuenta y ocho
59. fifty-nine is cincuenta y nueve
60. sixty is sesenta.
61. sixty-one is sesenta y uno
62. sixty-two is sesenta y dos
63. sixty-three is sesenta y tres
64. sixty-four is sesenta y cuatro
65. sixty-five is sesenta y cinco
66. sixty-six is sesenta y seis
67. sixty-seven is sesenta y siete
68. sixty-eight is sesenta y ocho
69. sixty-nine is sesenta y nueve

70. seventy is setenta
71. seventy-one is setenta y uno
72. seventy-two is setenta y dos
73. seventy-three is setenta y tres
74. seventy-four is setenta y cuatro
75. seventy-five is setenta y cinco
76. seventy-six is setenta y seis
77. seventy-seven is setenta y siete
78. seventy-eight is setenta y ocho
79. seventy-nine is setenta y nueve
80. eighty is ochenta
81. eighty-one is ochenta y uno
82. eighty-two is ochenta y dos
83. eighty-three is ochenta y tres
84. eighty-four is ochenta y cuatro
85. eighty-five is ochenta y cinco
86. eighty-six is ochenta y seis
87. eighty-seven is ochenta y siete
88. eighty-eight is ochenta y ocho
89. eighty-nine is ochenta y nueve
90. ninety is noventa
91. ninety-one is noventa y uno
92. ninety-two is noventa y dos
93. ninety-three is noventa y tres
94. ninety-four is noventa y cuatro
95. ninety-five is noventa y cinco
96. ninety-six is noventa y seis
97. ninety-seven is noventa y siete
98. ninety-eight is noventa y ocho
99. ninety- nine is noventa y nueve
100. one hundred is cien

Ordinal Numbers

1º	First is primero
2º	Second is segundo
3º	Third is tercero
4º	Fourth is cuarto
5º	Fifth is quinto
6º	Sixth is sexto
7º	Seventh is séptimo
8º	Eighth is octavo
9º	Ninth is noveno
10º	Tenth is décimo
11º	Eleventh is undécimo
12º	Twelfth is duodécimo
13º	Thirteenth is décimotercero
20º	Twentieth is vigésimo
30º	Thirtieth is trigésimo
40º	Fortieth is cuadragésimo
50º	Fiftieth is quincuagésimo
60º	Sixtieth is sexagésimo
70º	Seventieth is septuagésimo
80º	Eightieth is octogésimo
90º	Ninetieth is nonagésimo
100º	One hundredth is centésimo

Chapter 4: Places and Animals

Here is what popular animals and places are called in Spanish.

Let's start with animals.

Places and rooms

Airport is aeropuerto
Apartment is apartamento
Aquarium is acuario
Avenue is avenida
Bakery is panadería
Bank is banco
Bar is bar
Basement is sótano
Bathroom is baño
Bay is bahía
Beach is playa
Bookstore is librería
Bridge is puente
Building is edificio
Bus Station is estación de autobuses
Bus Stop is parada de autobuses
Cafe is cafetería
Cake Shop is pastelería
Castle is castillo
Cave is cueva
Cemetery is cementerio
Church is iglesia
Circus is circo
City is ciudad
Classroom is salón de clases
Clinic is clínica
Coast is costa
College is universidad
Company is compañía
Country is país
Countryside is campo
Court is tribunal
Dessert is desierto
Downtown is centro de la ciudad
East is este
Factory is fábrica
Farm is granja
Fire Station is estación de bomberos
Forest is bosque
Fruit shop is frutería
Garage is garaje
Gas Station is estación de servicio
Gym is gimnasio
Hairdressing Salon is peluquería
Home is hogar
Hospital is hospital
Hotel is hotel
House is casa
Ice cream Shop is heladería
Isle is isla

Kitchen is cocina
Laboratory is laboratorio
Lake is lago
Land is terreno
Library is biblioteca
Living room is sala de estar
Mall is centro comercial
Market is mercado
Mountain is montaña
Movie theatre is cine
Museum is museo
North is norte
Ocean is océano
Office is oficina
Park is parque
Parking lot is estacionamiento
Pharmacy is farmacia
Police station is estación de policía
Pool is piscina
Port is puerto
Prison/ jail is prisión/ cárcel
Restaurant is restaurante
River is río
Road is carretera
Room is habitación
School is escuela
Sea is mar
South is sur
Square is plaza
Stadium is estadio
State is estado
Store is tienda
Street is calle
Subway station is estación del metro
Supermarket is supermercado
Temple is templo
Theatre is teatro
Tower is torre
Town is pueblo
Train Station is estación de trenes
University is universidad
West is oeste
Workshop is taller
World is mundo
Zoo is zoológico

Animals

Anaconda is anaconda
Ant is hormiga
Antelope is antílope
Bear is oso
Beaver is castor
Bee is abeja
Beetle is escarabajo
Bird is ave
Boar is jabalí
Buffalo is búfalo
Bull is toro
Butterfly is mariposa
Cat is gato
Chameleon is camaleón
Chicken is gallina
Cobra is cobra
Cockroach is cucaracha
Cow is vaca
Crab is cangrejo
Cricket is grillo
Crocodile is cocodrilo
Deer is venado
Dog is perro
Dolphin is delfín
Donkey is burro
Dove is paloma
Dragonfly is libélula
Duck is pato
Eagle is águila
Elephant is elefante
Firefly is luciérnaga
Fish is pez
Flea is pulga
Fly is mosca

Frog is rana (female)/sapo (male)
Giraffe is jirafa
Goat is cabra
Goose is ganso
Gorilla is gorila
Grasshopper is saltamontes
Hamster is hámster
Hawk is halcón
Hippopotamus is hipopótamo
Horse is caballo
Hyena is hiena
Jellyfish is medusa
Kangaroo is canguro
Koala is koala
Leopard is leopardo
Lion is león
Lobster is langosta
Mole is topo
Monkey is mono
Mosquito is mosquito
Mouse is ratón
Octopus is pulpo
Ostrich is avestruz
Owl is búho
Parrot is loro
Pelican is pelícano
Penguin is pingüino
Pig is cerdo
Porcupine is puercoespín
Rabbit is conejo
Rat is rata
Raven is cuervo
Rhinoceros is rinoceronte

Rooster is gallo
Scorpion is escorpión
Seal is foca
Shark is tiburón
Sheep is oveja
Snake is serpiente
Spider is araña
Squirrel is ardilla
Starfish is estrella de mar
Swan is cisne
Termites is termitas

Tick is garrapata
Tiger is tigre
Toucan is tucán
Turkey is pavo
Turtle is Tortuga
Wasp is avispa
Whale is ballena
Wolf is lobo
Worm is gusano
Zebra is cebra

Chapter 5: Description, Clothes, Colors and Body Parts

Description and Clothes

Adult is adulto
Bad is malo
Bag pack is mochila
Bald is calvo
Beard is barba
Beautiful is bonito (a)
Belt is cinturón
Big is grande
Birthmark is lunar
Blond (e) is rubio
Blouse is blusa
Boots is botas
Bracelet is pulsera
Brunette is Moreno
Cap is gorra
Clothes is ropa
Coat is abrigo
Curly is rizado
Dress is vestido
Earrings is zarcillos/pendientes
Fat is gordo
Freckles is pecas
Glasses is lentes/gafas
Gloves is guantes
Good is bueno
Hat is sombrero
Heals is tacones
Jacket is chaqueta
Large is grande
Long is largo
Medium is mediano
Moustache is bigote
Necklace is collar
New is nuevo
Old is viejo
Pants is pantalones
Poor is pobre
Pretty is lindo (a)
Purse is cartera
Redhead is pelirrojo
Rich is rico
Ring is anillo
Sandals is sandalias
Scarf is bufanda
Shoes is zapatos
Short is corto
Shorts is shorts
Skirt is falda
Small is pequeño
Sneakers is zapatos deportivos
Socks is medias
Straight is liso
Suitcase is maleta
Sweater is suéter
T-shirt is camiseta
Tall is alto
Thin is delgado
Ugly is feo (a)
Underwear is ropa interior
Vest is chaleco
Watch is reloj
Young is joven

Colors

Aquamarine is aguamarina
Beige is beige
Black is negro
Blue is azul
Brown is marrón
Coral is coral
Cyan is cian
Fuchsia is fucsia
Gold is dorado
Green is verde
Grey is gris
Orange is anaranjado
Pink is rosado
Purple is morado
Red is rojo
Silver is plateado
Turquoise is turquesa
Violet is violeta
White is blanco
Yellow is amarillo

Body Parts

Abdomen is abdomen
Ankles is tobillos
Arms is brazos
Back is espalda
Bellybutton is ombligo
Blood is sangre
Bone is hueso
Brain is cerebro
Ear is oreja
Elbow is codo
Eyebrows is cejas
Eyelashes is pestañas
Eyes is ojos
Face is cara
Feet is pies
Fingers is dedos de las manos
Hair is cabello
Hands is manos
Head is cabeza
Heart is corazón
Knees is rodillas
Legs is piernas
Lips is labios
Lungs is pulmones
Mouth is boca
Muscle is músculo
Nails is uñas
Neck is cuello
Nose is nariz
Shoulders is hombros
Skin is piel
Stomach is estómago
Teeth is dientes
Thorax is tórax
Toes is Dedos de los pies
Tongue is lengua
Wrist is muñeca

Chapter 6: Food, Fruits and Vegetables

Almond is almendra
Apple is manzana
Artichoke is alcachofa
Bacon is tocino
Banana is plátano
Beer is cerveza
Bread is pan
Broccoli is brócoli
Bubblegum is chicle
Butter is mantequilla
Cabbage is repollo
Cake is pastel
Candies is golosinas
Carrot is zanahoria
Cauliflower is coliflor
Celery is apio
Cereal is cereal
Cheese is queso
Cherry is cereza
Chicken is pollo
Chocolate is chocolate
Coconut is coco
Coffee is café
Corn is maíz
Cucumber is pepino
Cupcake is cupcake/magdalena
Donuts is donut
Eggplant is berenjena
Eggs is huevos
Fish is pescado
Flour is harina
Garlic is ajo
Gelatin is gelatina

Ginger is jenjibre
Grapes is uvas
Ham is jamón
Hamburger is hamburguesa
Honey is miel
Hotdog is perro caliente
Ice cream is helado
Juice is jugo
Leek is puerro
Lemon is limón
Lettuce is lechuga
Lime is lima
Lollipop is chupete
Mango is mango
Marmalade is mermelada
Meat is carne
Milk is leche
Nut is nuez
Oil is aceite
Onion is cebolla
Orange is naranja
Papaya is papaya
Passion fruit is maracuyá
Pasta is pasta
Peach is durazno
Pear is pera
Peas is guisantes
Pepper is pimienta
Pickles is pepinillos
Pie is pastel
Pineapple is piña
Pizza is pizza
Plum is ciruela

Popcorn is palomitas
Potato is papa
Pumpkin is calabaza
Radishes is rábanos
Raspberry is frambuesa
Rum is ron
Salad is ensalada
Salt is sal
Sauce is salsa
Sausage is salchicha
Soda is gaseosa
Soup is sopa

Sprouts is coles
Strawberry is fresa
Sugar is azúcar
Sushi is sushi
Tea is té
Tomato is tomate
Vinegar is vinagre
Water is agua
Watermelon is sandía
Wine is vino
Yogurt is yogur

Chapter 7: Family and People

Anyone is nadie
Aunt is tía
Baby is bebé
Boss is jefe
Boy is varón
Boyfriend is novio
Brother is hermano
Child is niño
Classmate is compañero de clases
Colleague is colega
Couple is pareja
Cousin is primo, prima
Dad is papá
Daughter is hija
Everybody is todos
Everyone is todos
Father is padre
Friend is amigo
Girl is niña
Girlfriend is novia
Grandma is abuela
Grandpa is abuelo
Grandparents is abuelos
Guy is chico
He is él
Herself is si misma
Him is él
Himself is él mismo
Husband is esposo
I is yo
It is eso
Itself is si mismo
Kid is niño
Lover is amante
Man is hombre
Married is casado
Miss is señora
Mister is señor
Mom is mamá
Mother is madre
Myself is mí mismo
Neighbor is vecino
Nephew is sobrino
Niece is sobrina
Parents is padres
Partner is compañero
People is gente
Person is persona
Pet is mascota
Roommate is compañero de habitación
Secretary is secretaria
She is ella
Siblings is hermanos
Single is soltero
Sister is hermana
Someone is alguien
Son is hijo
Them is ellos, ellas
Themselves is ellos mismos
They is ellos, ellas
Uncle is tío
Us is nosotros
We is nosotros
Wife is esposa
Woman is mujer
You is tú
Yourself is tú mismo

Chapter 8: Feelings and Emotions

Amazement is asombro
Anger is ira
Ansiety is ansiedad
Arrogance is arrogancia
Believe is creer
Bravery is valentía
Confidence is seguridad
Confused is confundido
Depressed is deprimido
Disappointment is decepción
Empathy is empatía
Energetic is enérgico
Enthusiasm is entusiasmo
Envy is envidia
Excitement is emoción
Fear is miedo
Frustration is frustración
Happiness is felicidad
Hate is odio
Honesty is honestidad
Hope is esperanza
Intrigue is intriga
Jealousy is celos
Joy is alegría
Kindness is bondad
Laziness is pereza
Lie is mentir
Love is amor
Lust is lujuria
Modesty is humildad
Motivation is motivación
Optimism is optimismo
Passion is pasión

Patience is paciencia
Peace is paz
Pride is orgullo
Resentment is rencor
Respect is respeto
Sadness is tristeza
Shame is vergüenza
Shyness is timidez
Sorrow is dolor
Stress is estrés
Worry is preocupación

Chapter 9: Sports and Activities

Draw is dibujar
Paint is colorear
Badminton is bádminton
Baseball is béisbol
Basketball is baloncesto
Biking is ciclismo
Boxing is boxeo
Browse the internet is navegar en internet
Climb is escalar
Cricket is críquet
Dance is bailar
Dive is bucear
Football is fútbol
Game is juego
Go Fishing is ir de pesca
Go shopping is ir de compras
Golf is golf
Gymnastics is gimnasia
Handball is balonmano
Hockey is hockey
Play a musical instrument is tocar un instrumento musical
Play is jugar
Play videogames is jugar videojuegos
Read is leer
Rugby is rugby
Run is correr
Sing is cantar
Ski is esquí
Surf is surfear
Swim is nadar
Tennis is tenis
Volleyball is vóleibol
Walk is caminar
Waterpolo is waterpolo
Walk is caminar
Waterpolo is waterpolo
Wrestling is lucha
Write is escribir

Chapter 10: Professions

Actor is actor
Actress is actriz
Administrator is administrador
Architect is arquitecto
Artist is artista
Athlete is atleta, deportista
Babysitter is niñera
Bodyguard is guardaespaldas
Botanist is botánico
Dentist is dentista
Designer is diseñador
Doctor is doctor
Driver is chofer
Editor is editor
Employee is empleado
Engineer is ingeniero
Firefighter is bombero
Florist is florista
Hairstylist is estilista
Journalist is periodista
Judge is juez
Lawyer is abogado
Makeup Artist is maquillador
Manager is gerente
Mechanic is mecánico
Miner is minero
Nurse is enfermera
Paramedic is paramédico
Photographer is fotógrafo
Physicist is físico
Pilot is piloto
Player is jugador
Police officer is oficial de policía
Producer is productor
Professor is profesor
Scientist is científico
Stewardess is azafata
Student is estudiante
Teacher is maestro
Translator is traductor
Veterinarian is veterinario
Writer is escritor

Chapter 11: Countries and Nationalities

American is estadounidense
Argentine is Argentina
Argentinean is argentino (a)
Australia is Australia
Australian is australiano
Belgian is belga
Belgium is Bélgica
Bolivia is Bolivia
Bolivian is boliviano, boliviana
Brazil is Brasil
Brazilian is brasileño, brasileña
Cameroon is Camerún
Cameroonian is camerunés, camerunesa
Canada is Canadá
Canadian is canadiense
Chile is Chile
Chilean is chileno, chilena
China is China
Chinese is chino, china
Colombia is Colombia
Colombian is colombiano, colombiana
Costa Rica is Costa Rica
Costarican is costaricense
Croatia is Croacia
Croatian is croata
Danish is danés, danesa
Denmark is Dinamarca
Egypt is Egipto
Egyptian is egipcio/egipcia
England is Inglaterra
English is inglés, inglesa
France is Francia
French is francés, francesa

German is alemán, alemana
Germany is Alemania
Ghana is Ghana
Ghanaian is ghanés, ghanesa
Haiti is Haití
Haitian is haitiano, haitiana
India is India
Indian is indio, india
Ireland is Irlanda
Irish is irlandés, irlandesa
Italian is italiano, italiana
Italy is Italia
Jamaica is Jamaica
Jamaican is jamaiquino, jamaiquina
Japan is Japón
Japanese is japonés, japonesa
Malaysia is Malasia
Malaysian is malasio, malasia
Mexican is mexicano, mexicana
Mexico is México
Moroccan is marroquí
Morocco is Marruecos
New Zealand is neozelandés, neozelandesa
New Zealand is Nueva Zelanda
Nigeria is Nigeria
Nigerian is nigeriano, nigeriana
North Korea is Corea del Norte
North Korean is norcoreano, norcoreana
Peru is Perú
Peruvian is peruano, peruana
Portugal is Portugal
Portuguese is Portugués, portuguesa
Russia is Rusia
Russian is ruso, rusa
Scotland is Escocia
Scottish is escocés, escocesa

South Africa is Sudáfrica
South African is sudafricano, sudafricana
South Korea is Corea del Sur
South Korean is surcoreano, surcoreana
Spain is España
Spanish is español, española
Sweden is Suecia
Swedish is sueco, sueca
Swiss is suizo, suiza
Switzerland is Suiza
Ukraine is Ucrania
Ukrainian is ucraniano, ucraniana
United States is Estados Unidos
Venezuela is Venezuela
Venezuelan is venezolano, venezolana

Chapter 12: Cognates

Cognates are words that have the same meaning, and have the same or a similar spelling in two different languages. Here are some of them:

1. Ability is habilidad
2. Accept is aceptar
3. Accident is accidente
4. Acid is ácido
5. Acne is acné
6. Act is actuar
7. Action is acción
8. Active is activo
9. Activity is actividad
10. Actual is actual
11. Administration is administración
12. Admirable is admirable
13. Admiration is admiración
14. Affect is afectar
15. Agency is agencia
16. Alarm is alarma
17. Alcoholic is alcóholico
18. Altar is altar
19. Alucination is alucinación
20. Analysis is análisis
21. Annex is anexo
22. Anonymous is anónimo
23. Antenna is antena
24. Antonym is antónimo
25. Arbitrary is arbitrario
26. Archaic is arcáico
27. Archives is archivos
28. Area is área
29. Arrest is arrestar
30. Art is arte

31. Artificial is artificial
32. Artist is artista
33. Artistic is artístico
34. Association is asociación
35. Attack is ataque
36. Attention is atención
37. Attractive is atractivo
38. Author is autor
39. Authority is autoridad
40. Automobile is automóvil
41. Bacteria is bacteria
42. Barbarism is barbarismo
43. Base is base
44. Benefit is beneficio
45. Biography is biografía
46. Cable is cable
47. Calculator is calculadora
48. Calm is calma
49. Camera is cámara
50. Cancer is cáncer
51. Candidate is candidato
52. Capacity is capacidad
53. Capital is capital
54. Capture is capturar
55. Car is coche
56. Cardinal is cardinal
57. Caricature is caricatura
58. Case is caso
59. Casino is casino
60. Cause is causa
61. Cent is céntimo
62. Center is centro
63. Centimeter is centímetro
64. Central is central
65. Ceramic is cerámica
66. Ceremony is ceremonia
67. Character is carácter

68. Circular is circular
69. Circulation is circulación
70. Civil is civil
71. Civilization is civilización
72. Class is clase
73. Classic is clásico
74. Client is cliente
75. Clone is clonar
76. Club is club
77. Colloquial is coloquial
78. Combination is combinación
79. Combine is combinar
80. Common is común
81. Company is compañía
82. Compare is comparar
83. Competition is competición
84. Complement is complementar
85. Complicated is complicado
86. Comprehensive is comprensivo
87. Conclusion is conclusión
88. Condition is condición
89. Conference is conferencia
90. Confirm is confirmar
91. Congress is congreso
92. Connect is conectar
93. Consider is considerar
94. Consistent is consistente
95. Consonant is consonante
96. Continent is continente
97. Continue is continuar
98. Contradiction is contradicción
99. Contrast is contraste
100. Control is control
101. Convention is convención
102. Corruption is corrupción
103. Cost is costar
104. Courtesy is cortesía

105. Crime is crimen
106. Criminal is criminal
107. Crisis is crisis
108. Cristal is cristal
109. Critic is crítico
110. Cruel is cruel
111. Cultural is cultural
112. Culture is cultura
113. Data is datos
114. Debate is debate
115. Decade is década
116. Decide is decidir
117. Decimal is decimal
118. Decision is decisión
119. Decorate is decorar
120. Defect is defecto
121. Defense is defensa
122. Democracy is democracia
123. Dental is dental
124. Dependence is dependencia
125. Deport is deportar
126. Deposit is depósito
127. Describe is describir
128. Destiny is destino
129. Determine is determinar
130. Dictionary is diccionario
131. Different is diferente
132. Digital is digital
133. Diploma is diploma
134. Direction is dirección
135. Director is director
136. Distance is distancia
137. Diversity is diversidad
138. Document is documento
139. Dollar is dólar
140. Donation is donación
141. Dragon is dragón

142. Drama is drama
143. Dynamic is dinámico
144. Economy is economía
145. Education is educación
146. Effect is efecto
147. Election is elección
148. Electronic is electrónico
149. Eliminate is eliminar
150. Emergency is emergencia
151. Energy is energía
152. Enigma is enigma
153. Enter is entrar
154. Error is error
155. Etcetera is etcétera
156. Euro is euro
157. Event is evento
158. Evidence is evidencia
159. Evolution is evolución
160. Exact is exacto
161. Exam is examen
162. Excellent is excelente
163. Exclusive is exclusivo
164. Excuse is excusa
165. Experience is experiencia
166. Experimental is experimental
167. Expert is experto
168. Express is expreso
169. Expression is expresión
170. Extra is extra
171. Extreme is extremo
172. Factor is factor
173. Famous is famoso
174. Fanatic is fanático
175. Favor is favor
176. Favorite is favorito
177. Federal is federal
178. Feminine is femenino

179. Festival is festival
180. Fiction is ficción
181. Figure is figura
182. Figure is figura
183. Final is final
184. Financial is financiero
185. Firm is firme
186. Flexibility is flexibilidad
187. Flexible is flexible
188. Form is forma
189. Formal is formal
190. Format is formato
191. Fortune is fortuna
192. Forum is foro
193. Funeral is funeral
194. Fusion is fusión
195. Future is futuro
196. Galaxy is galaxia
197. General is general
198. Generation is generación
199. Global is global
200. Guardian is guardián
201. History is historia
202. Honor is honor
203. Horizon is horizonte
204. Human is humano
205. Humor is humor
206. Hybrid is híbrido
207. Hypothesis is hipótesis
208. Iconic is icónico
209. Idea is idea
210. Ideology is ideología
211. Idiot is idiota
212. Idol is ídolo
213. Ignore is ignorar
214. Illumination is iluminación
215. Illusionist is ilusionista

216. Image is imagen
217. Imagination is imaginación
218. Imagine is imaginar
219. Imitation is imitación
220. Immediate is inmediato
221. Immigration is inmigración
222. Immune is inmune
223. Impact is impacto
224. Important is importante
225. Impossible is imposible
226. Include is incluir
227. Indicate is indicar
228. Individual is individual
229. Industrial is industrial
230. Industry is industria
231. Information is información
232. Innocence is inocencia
233. Innovation is innovación
234. Insects is insectos
235. Institution is institución
236. Insult is insulto
237. Integral is integral
238. Intelligence is inteligencia
239. Interest is interés
240. Interfere is interferir
241. International is internacional
242. Internet is internet
243. Introduction is introducción
244. Invent is inventar
245. Invisible is invisible
246. Justice is justicia
247. Juvenile is juvenil
248. Kilogram is kilogramo
249. Legal is legal
250. Legion is legión
251. Liberal is liberal
252. Liberty is libertad

253. Limit is límite
254. Line is línea
255. Liquid is líquido
256. List is lista
257. Literal is literal
258. Literature is literatura
259. Local is local
260. Local is local
261. Lotion is loción
262. Magic is magia
263. Magnetism is magnetismo
264. Magnitude is magnitud
265. Manual is manual
266. Map is mapa
267. Masculine is masculino
268. Material is material
269. Maximum is máximo
270. Media is medios
271. Medic is médico
272. Medical is médico
273. Medicine is medicina
274. Meditation is meditación
275. Memory is memoria
276. Mental is mental
277. Mention is mención
278. Menu is menú
279. Metal is metal
280. Metaphor is metáfora
281. Method is método
282. Meticulous is meticuloso
283. Military is militar
284. Million is millón
285. Mineral is mineral
286. Minimalism is minimalismo
287. Minimum is mínimo
288. Minute is minuto
289. Model is modelo

290. Modern is moderno
291. Moment is momento
292. Monologue is monólogo
293. Monotony is monotonía
294. Moral is moral
295. Mortal is mortal
296. Motor is motor
297. Multiple is múltiple
298. Music is música
299. Nation is nación
300. National is nacional
301. Natural is natural
302. Necessary is necesario
303. Negative is negativo
304. No is no
305. Note is nota
306. Novel is novela
307. Obedient is obediente
308. Object is objeto
309. Objective is objetivo
310. Obligation is obligación
311. Obscene is obsceno
312. Observe is observar
313. Obtuse is obtuso
314. Obvious is obvio
315. Occasion is ocasión
316. Official is oficial
317. Operation is operación
318. Opportunity is oportunidad
319. Optical is óptico
320. Order is orden
321. Ordinary is ordinario
322. Organism is organismo
323. Organization is organización
324. Origin is origen
325. Original is original
326. Ovation is ovación

327. Oxygen is oxígeno
328. Panic is pánico
329. Paper is papel
330. Paradigm is paradigma
331. Parallel is paralelo
332. Pardon is perdón
333. Part is parte
334. Particular is particular
335. Pass is pasar
336. Peculiar is peculiar
337. Perfect is perfecto
338. Perfection is perfección
339. Perfume is perfume
340. Period is período
341. Permanent is permanente
342. Person is persona
343. Personal is personal
344. Photo is foto
345. Piano is piano
346. Piece is pieza
347. Pine is pino
348. Plan is plan
349. Planet is planeta
350. Plant is planta
351. Plural is plural
352. Poem is poema
353. Polemic is polémica
354. Political is político
355. Politics is política
356. Popular is popular
357. Position is posición
358. Positive is positivo
359. Possible is posible
360. Potion is poción
361. Practice is practicar
362. Preface is prefacio
363. Preparation is preparación

364. Prepare is preparar
365. Prescription is prescripción
366. Present is presente
367. President is presidente
368. Principle is principio
369. Private is privado
370. Problem is problema
371. Process is proceso
372. Produce is producir
373. Product is producto
374. Production is producción
375. Products is productos
376. Program is programa
377. Project is proyecto
378. Propaganda is propaganda
379. Protagonist is protagonista
380. Protection is protección
381. Public is público
382. Pulse is pulso
383. Pure is puro
384. Radical is radical
385. Radio is radio
386. Ramification is ramificación
387. Real is real
388. Recent is reciente
389. Record is récord
390. Reduce is reducir
391. Reference is referencia
392. Region is región
393. Regular is regular
394. Relation is relación
395. Religion is religión
396. Remove is remover
397. Repetition is repetición
398. Represent is representar
399. Republic is república
400. Resist is resistir

401. Result is resultado
402. Reunion is reunión
403. Revolver is revólver
404. Rob is robar
405. Rock is roca
406. Role is rol
407. Romantic is romántico
408. Salsa is salsa
409. Salute is saludo
410. Sardine is sardina
411. Satellite is satélite
412. Scene is escena
413. Secret is secreto
414. Section is sección
415. Security is seguridad
416. Selection is selección
417. Semantic is semántica
418. Sentiment is sentimiento
419. Separate is separar
420. Serie is serie
421. Serious is serio
422. Service is servicio
423. Session is sesión
424. Severe is severo
425. Sex is sexo
426. Sexual is sexual
427. Significant is significativo
428. Silence is silencio
429. Similar is similar
430. Simple is simple
431. Simulator is simulador
432. Singular is singular
433. Site is sitio
434. Situation is situación
435. Social is social
436. Society is sociedad
437. Sofa is sofá

438. Solid is sólido
439. Solution is solución
440. Sonorous is sonoro
441. Space is espacio
442. Special is especial
443. Specific is específico
444. Spiral is espiral
445. Spirit is espíritu
446. Strategy estrategia
447. Structure is estructura
448. Studio is estudio
449. Stupid is estúpido
450. Subjective is subjetivo
451. Supplement is suplemento
452. Supreme is supremo
453. Synonym is sinónimo
454. Technology is tecnología
455. Television is televisión
456. Temperature is temperatura
457. Terminal is terminal
458. Terrible is terrible
459. Terror is terror
460. Theory is teoría
461. Total is total
462. Tourist is turista
463. Traditional is tradicional
464. Traffic is tráfico
465. Triple is triple
466. Uniform is uniforme
467. Union is unión
468. Unit is unidad
469. Universal is universal
470. Universe is universo
471. Urgent is urgente
472. Urn is urna
473. Use is usar
474. Usual is usual

475. Vagina is vagina
476. Vanilla is vainilla
477. Vapor is vapor
478. Various is varios
479. Venom is veneno
480. Ventilator is ventilador
481. Verb is verbo
482. Versatile is versátil
483. Vertical is vertical
484. Vertigo is vértigo
485. Veteran is veterano
486. Victory is victoria
487. Violence is violencia
488. Violin is violín
489. Virile is viril
490. Virtual is virtual
491. Virtue is virtud
492. Virus is virus
493. Visible is visible
494. Vision is visión
495. Visit is visitar
496. Visual is visual
497. Volume is volumen
498. Voluntary is voluntario
499. Vomit is vómito
500. Zone is zona

Chapter 13: 1000 Most Used Words

We will start by saying the English word first, followed by the Spanish!

1. A is un
2. Able is capaz
3. About is acerca de
4. Above is por encima de
5. Abroad is en el extranjero
6. Absolute is absoluto
7. Absorb is absorber
8. Abstract is abstracto
9. Abundance is abundancia
10. Academic is académico
11. Access is acceso
12. Accomplish is cumplir
13. According is acorde
14. Account is cuenta
15. Accurate is preciso
16. Achieve is lograr
17. Across is a través
18. Adapt is adaptarse
19. Add is agregar
20. Address is dirección
21. Admire is admirar
22. Adrenaline is adrenalina
23. Advantage is ventaja
24. Adventure is aventura
25. Advertising is publicidad
26. After is después
27. Again is otra vez
28. Against is contra
29. Age is edad
30. Ago is hace
31. Agree is estar de acuerdo

32. Agreement is contrato
33. Airplane is avión
34. All is todo
35. Alliance is alianza
36. Allow is permitir
37. Almost is casi
38. Along is a lo largo de
39. Alphabet is abecedario
40. Already is ya
41. Also is también
42. Alternative is alternativa
43. Although is aunque
44. Always is siempre
45. Among is entre
46. Amount is cantidad
47. And is y
48. Anniversary is aniversario
49. Another is otro
50. Answer is responder
51. Any is ningún
52. Anything is nada
53. Appear is aparecer
54. Application is aplicación
55. Apply is aplicar
56. Appointment is cita
57. Approach is enfoque
58. Argue is argumentar
59. Argument is argumento
60. Army is ejército
61. Around is alrededor
62. Arrange is concertar
63. Arrive is llegar
64. Arrow is flecha
65. Article is artículo
66. As is como
67. Ask is preguntar

68. Assault is asalto
69. At is en
70. Attitude is actitud
71. Audience is audiencia
72. Audiovisual is audiovisual
73. Available is disponible
74. Average is promedio
75. Avoid is evitar
76. Award is premio
77. Awareness is conciencia
78. Away is lejos
79. Bachelor is licenciatura
80. Back is atrás
81. Background is trasfondo
82. Balance is equilibrio
83. Ball is pelota
84. Band is banda
85. Battery is batería
86. Be is ser/ estar
87. Bear is soportar
88. Because is porque
89. Become is convertirse
90. Bed is cama
91. Before is antes
92. Begin is empezar
93. Behaviour is comportamiento
94. Behind is detrás
95. Bell is campana
96. Bend is doblar
97. Best is mejor
98. Better is mejor
99. Between is entre
100. Beyond is más allá
101. Bike is bicicleta
102. Bill is factura
103. Birth is nacimiento

104. Birthday is cumpleaños
105. Bite is moder
106. Blame is culpa
107. Blow is soplar
108. Board is pizarra
109. Boat is barco
110. Book is libro
111. Bore is aburrir
112. Both is ambos
113. Bottle is botella
114. Bottom is fondo
115. Box is caja
116. Braid is trenza
117. Break is romper
118. Breakfast is desayuno
119. Breathe is respirar
120. Brick is ladrillo
121. Brilliant is brillante
122. Bring is traer
123. Brush is cepillo
124. Build is construir
125. Burn is quemar
126. Business is negocio
127. But is pero
128. Buy is comprar
129. By is por
130. Call is llamar
131. Campaign is campaña
132. Can is poder
133. Cancel is cancelar
134. Card is tarjeta
135. Care is cuidar
136. Career is carrera
137. Carry is llevar
138. Cash is efectivo
139. Cast is reparto

140. Catch is atrapar
141. Cell is celda
142. Cellphone is celular
143. Century is siglo
144. Certain is cierto
145. Certainly is verdaderamente
146. Chain is cadena
147. Chair is silla
148. Challenge is desafío
149. Champion is campeón
150. Chance is oportunidad
151. Change is cambiar
152. Channel is canal
153. Characteristic is característica
154. Charge is cobrar
155. Charger is cargador
156. Charity is caridad
157. Chart is tabla
158. Check is chequear
159. Chemistry is química
160. Childhood is infancia
161. Choice is elección
162. Choose is elegir
163. Christmas is navidad
164. Claim is reclamar
165. Clean is limpiar
166. Clear is claro
167. Clearly is claramente
168. Close is cerca
169. Code is código
170. Collapse is colapsar
171. Collection is colección
172. Comb is peinarse
173. Come is venir
174. Comedy is comedia
175. Comfort is comodidad

176. Comment is comentar
177. Commercial is comercial
178. Compare is comparar
179. Compete is competir
180. Complain is quejarse
181. Complex is complejo
182. Compound is compuesto
183. Computer is computadora
184. Concentrate is concentrarse
185. Concern is preocupar
186. Concert is concierto
187. Congratulations is felicitaciones
188. Conjugate is conjugar
189. Consequence is consecuencia
190. Consult is consultar
191. Contacts is contactos
192. Contain is contener
193. Contamination is contaminación
194. Context is contexto
195. Contribution is contribución
196. Controversy is controversia
197. Cook is cocinar
198. Cough is toser
199. Could is podría
200. Count is contar
201. Courage is coraje
202. Course is curso
203. Cover is cubrir
204. Craft is manualidad
205. Craziness is locura
206. Create is crear
207. Crew is equipo
208. Cross is cruzar
209. Cry is llorar
210. Cup is copa
211. Curiosity is curiosidad

212. Current is actual
213. Curve is curva
214. Customer is cliente
215. Cut is cortar
216. Cycle is ciclo
217. Damage is daño
218. Danger is peligro
219. Dark is oscuro
220. Dead is muerte
221. Deal is trato
222. Death is muerte
223. Deep is profundo
224. Definition is definición
225. Degree is título universitario
226. Delivery is envío
227. Demand is exigir
228. Deny is negar
229. Departure is salida
230. Desire is desear
231. Desk is escritorio
232. Despite is a pesar de
233. Detail is detallar
234. Detect is detectar
235. Develop is desarrollar
236. Development is desarrollo
237. Device is dispositivo
238. Die is morir
239. Diet is dieta
240. Difficult is difícil
241. Dig is cavar
242. Dimension is dimensión
243. Dinner is cena
244. Dirt is suciedad
245. Disappear is desaparecer
246. Disaster is desastre
247. Discipline is disciplina

248. Discount is descuento
249. Discover is descubrir
250. Discuss is discutir
251. Disease is enfermedad
252. Dish is plato
253. Dispute is disputa
254. Dissolve is disolver
255. Distinction is distinción
256. Divorce is divorcio
257. Do is hacer
258. Domestic is doméstico
259. Dominate is dominar
260. Door is puerta
261. Doubt is dudar
262. Down is abajo
263. Download is descargar
264. Dozen is docena
265. Draft is borrador
266. Dream is sueño
267. Drink is beber
268. Drive is conducir
269. Drop is gota
270. Drown is ahogarse
271. Drug is droga
272. Dry is secar
273. Dubbing is doblaje
274. During is durante
275. Dust is polvo
276. Dyslexia is dislexia
277. Each is cada
278. Early is temprano
279. Earn is ganar
280. Earthquake is terremoto
281. Easy is fácil
282. Eat is comer
283. Edge is borde

284. Efficiency is eficiencia
285. Effort is esfuerzo
286. Either is cualquiera
287. Elastic is elástico
288. Elegance is elegancia
289. Else is además
290. Email is correo electrónico
291. Embassy is embajada
292. Emphasize is enfatizar
293. End is final
294. Engine is motor
295. Enjoy is disfrutar
296. Enough is suficiente
297. Enterprise is empresa
298. Entertainment is entretenimiento
299. Entire is entero
300. Entrance is entrada
301. Environment is ambiente
302. Episode is episodio
303. Equipment is equipamiento
304. Eraser is borrador
305. Escape is escapar
306. Especially is especialmente
307. Essay is ensayo
308. Establish is establecer
309. Ethics is ética
310. Evaluate is evaluar
311. Even is sin embargo
312. Ever is jamás
313. Every is cada
314. Everything is todo
315. Exaggerate is exagerar
316. Example is ejemplo
317. Exchange is intercambio
318. Executive is ejecutivo
319. Exhibit is exhibir

320. Expand is expandir
321. Expect is esperar
322. Expensive is costoso
323. Expire is expirar
324. Explain is explicar
325. Fact is hecho
326. Fail is fallar
327. Fall is caer
328. Fantasy is fantasía
329. Far is lejos
330. Fast is rápido
331. Feature is característica
332. Fee is tarifa
333. Feed is alimentar
334. Feedback is observaciones
335. Feel is sentir
336. Fever is fiebre
337. Few is pocos
338. Fibber is fibra
339. Field is terreno
340. Fight is pelea
341. File is archivo
342. Fill is llenar
343. Film is filmar
344. Filter is filtro
345. Finally is finalmente
346. Find is encontrar
347. Fine is bien
348. Finish is terminar
349. Fire is fuego
350. Fit is caber
351. Fix is reparar
352. Flag is bandera
353. Flashlight is linterna
354. Flight is vuelo
355. Floor is piso

356. Flower is flor
357. Fly is volar
358. Focus is enfocar
359. Follow is seguir
360. For is para
361. Forbid is prohibir
362. Force is fuerza
363. Foreign is extranjero
364. Forget is olvidar
365. Former is antiguo
366. Formula is fórmula
367. Forward is avanzar
368. Fountain is fuente
369. Frame is cuadro
370. Free is gratis
371. Freedom is libertad
372. Friendship is amistad
373. From is de
374. Fuel is combustible
375. Full is lleno
376. Fun is diversión
377. Gentleman is caballero
378. Get is obtener
379. Ghost is fantasma
380. Gift is regalo
381. Give is dar
382. Glass is vidrio
383. Go is ir
384. Goal is meta
385. Government is gobierno
386. Grade is grado
387. Grammar is gramática
388. Great is genial
389. Ground is suelo
390. Group is grupo
391. Grow is crecer

392. Guess is adivinar
393. Guide is guíar
394. Gun is pistola
395. Habit is hábito
396. Half is mitad
397. Hang is colgar
398. Happen is suceder
399. Hard is duro/ difícil
400. Have is tener
401. Headline is titular
402. Health is salud
403. Hear is oír
404. Heavy is pesado
405. Helicopter is helicóptero
406. Hell is infierno
407. Help is ayudar
408. Her is su
409. Here is aquí
410. Hero is héroe
411. Hide is esconder
412. High is alto
413. Highlight is resaltar
414. His is su
415. Hit is golpear
416. Hold is aguantar
417. Holiday is vacaciones
418. Holy is sagrado
419. Homework is tarea
420. Hook is gancho
421. Host is antifrión
422. Hour is hora
423. How is cómo
424. However is sin embargo
425. Huge is enorme
426. Hunt is cazar
427. Hurt is lastimar

428. Ice is hielo
429. Identification is identificación
430. Identify is identificar
431. If is si
432. Illegal is ilegal
433. Illustrate is ilustrar
434. Immigrant is immigrante
435. Improve is mejorar
436. In is en
437. Income is ingresos
438. Increase is aumentar
439. Indeed is en efecto
440. Independence is independencia
441. Influence is influencia
442. Initiative is iniciativa
443. Inside is dentro
444. Inspection is inspección
445. Install is instalar
446. Instance is instancia
447. Instant is instante
448. Instead is en lugar de
449. Insurance is seguro de vida
450. Interface is interfaz
451. Interpretation is interpretación
452. Interview is entrevista
453. Into is en
454. Invest is invertir
455. Invite is invitar
456. Involve is involucrar
457. Iron is hierro
458. Issue is asunto
459. Itinerary is itinerario
460. Its is su
461. Jar is jarra
462. Job is trabajo
463. Join is unir

464. Joke is broma
465. Jump is saltar
466. Just is solamente
467. Justify is justificar
468. Keep is seguir
469. Key is llave
470. Keyboard is teclado
471. Kill is matar
472. King is rey
473. Knife is cuchillo
474. Knot is nudo
475. Know is saber
476. Knowledge is conocimiento
477. Lack is carencia
478. Language is idioma
479. Laser is láser
480. Last is último
481. Late is tarde
482. Later is más tarde
483. Laugh is reír
484. Law is ley
485. Lay is colocar
486. Lead is liderar
487. Leader is líder
488. League is liga
489. Lean is inclinarse
490. Learn is aprender
491. Least is menos
492. Leave is dejar
493. Lecture is conferencia
494. Left is izquierda
495. Legacy is legado
496. Legend is leyenda
497. Less is menos
498. Let is permitir
499. Letter is carta

500. Level is nivel
501. License is licencia
502. Life is vida
503. Light is luz
504. Like is gustar
505. Likely is probable
506. Linguistics is lingüística
507. Listen is escuchar
508. Live is vivir
509. Log is registrar
510. Logic is lógica
511. Look is mirar
512. Lose is perder
513. Lot is montón
514. Low is bajo
515. Luck is suerte
516. Luggage is equipaje
517. Lunch is almuerzo
518. Magazine is revista
519. Mail is correo
520. Main is principal
521. Maintain is mantener
522. Major is maestría
523. Make is hacer
524. Manage is dirigir
525. Management is gerencia
526. Many is mucho
527. Market is mercado
528. Marriage is matrimonio
529. Match is coincidir
530. Math is matemáticas
531. Matter is materia
532. Maximum is máximo
533. May is podría
534. Maybe is quizás
535. Me is yo

536. Mean is significar
537. Meaning is significado
538. Measure is medida
539. Meet is conocer
540. Meeting is reunión
541. Member is miembro
542. Message is mensaje
543. Microphone is micrófono
544. Middle is medio
545. Might is podría
546. Mind is mente
547. Minimum is mínimo
548. Mirror is espejo
549. Mistake is equivocarse
550. Mixture is mezcla
551. Money is dinero
552. Monitor is monitor
553. Mood is estado de ánimo
554. More is más
555. Most is más
556. Move is mover
557. Movement is movimiento
558. Movie is película
559. Much is mucho
560. Must is deber
561. My is mi
562. Mystery is misterio
563. Name is nombre
564. Near is cerca
565. Need is necesitar
566. Negotiate is negociar
567. Network is red
568. Never is nunca
569. News is noticias
570. Next is siguiente
571. Nice is agradable

572. Noise is ruido
573. Nominate is nominar
574. Not is no
575. Nothing is nada
576. Now is ahora
577. Number is número
578. Occur is ocurrir
579. Odd is raro
580. Of is de
581. Off is apagado
582. Offer is ofrecer
583. Often is a menudo
584. On is encima
585. Once is una vez
586. Only is único
587. Onto is a/ en/ sobre
588. Open is abrir
589. Or is o
590. Organic is orgánico
591. Organize is ordenar
592. Other is otro
593. Our is nuestro
594. Out is fuera
595. Outside is exterior
596. Oven is horno
597. Over is encima
598. Overwhelm is abrumar
599. Own is propio
600. Page is página
601. Pain is dolor
602. Paragraph is párrafo
603. Participate is participar
604. Party is fiesta
605. Passenger is pasajero
606. Passport is pasaporte
607. Password is contraseña

608. Past is pasado
609. Paste is pegar
610. Pay is pagar
611. Payment is pago
612. Peace is paz
613. Pencil is lápiz
614. Percentage is porcentaje
615. Perception is percepción
616. Perform is desempeñar
617. Performance is desempeño
618. Perhaps is quizás
619. Permanent is permanente
620. Permission is permiso
621. Personality is personalidad
622. Persuade is persuadir
623. Philosophy is filosofía
624. Phone is teléfono
625. Phrase is frase
626. Pick is elegir
627. Picture is imagen
628. Pillow is almohada
629. Plastic is plástico
630. Platform is plataforma
631. Point is punto
632. Policy is normativa
633. Population is población
634. Possession is posesión
635. Possibility is posibilidad
636. Pot is olla
637. Power is poder
638. Precaution is precaución
639. Predict is predecir
640. Preference is preferencia
641. Pregnancy is embarazo
642. Preserve is preservar
643. Press is prensa

644. Pressure is presión
645. Price is precio
646. Print is imprimir
647. Profile is perfil
648. Programming is programar
649. Promise is promesa
650. Pronunciation is pronunciación
651. Property is propiedad
652. Proposal is propuesta
653. Protein is proteína
654. Prove is probar
655. Provide is proveer
656. Psychology is psicología
657. Pull is tirar
658. Punctuality is puntualidad
659. Purchase is comprar
660. Push is empujar
661. Put is poner
662. Qualifications is calificaciones
663. Quality is calidad
664. Quantity is cantidad
665. Queen is reina
666. Question is pregunta
667. Quickly is rápidamente
668. Quit is renunciar
669. Quite is bastante
670. Quote is frase
671. Race is carrera
672. Rainbow is arcoiris
673. Raise is criar
674. Range is rango
675. Rate is tasa/tarifa
676. Rather is preferir
677. Reach is alcanzar
678. Reaction is reacción
679. Ready is listo

680. Reality is realidad
681. Realize is darse cuenta
682. Really is realmente
683. Reason is razón
684. Receive is recibir
685. Recently is recientemente
686. Recognize is reconocer
687. Recommend is recomendar
688. Recycle is reciclar
689. Reflect is reflexionar
690. Reflection is reflexión
691. Relief is alivio
692. Remain is permanecer
693. Remember is recordar
694. Repair is reparar
695. Replacement is reemplazo
696. Reply is contestar
697. Reputation is reputación
698. Require is requerir
699. Research is investigación
700. Reservation is reserva
701. Resource is recurso
702. Respond is responder
703. Response is respuesta
704. Rest is descansar
705. Restriction is restricción
706. Return is regresar
707. Reveal is revelar
708. Revolution is revolución
709. Reward is recompensa
710. Ribbon is lazo
711. Ride is recorrido
712. Right is derecha/ correcto
713. Rise is ascender
714. Risk is riesgo
715. Routine is rutina

716. Rule is regla
717. Rush is apuro
718. Safety is seguridad
719. Sale is venta
720. Same is igual
721. Sanction is sancionar
722. Sand is arena
723. Satisfaction is satisfacción
724. Savage is salvaje
725. Save is guardar
726. Savings is ahorros
727. Say is decir
728. Scale is escala
729. Scan is escanear
730. Scene is escena
731. Schedule is horario
732. Scheme is esquema
733. Scholarship is beca
734. Science is ciencia
735. Scissors is tijeras
736. Scratch is rasguñar
737. Scream is gritar
738. Screen is pantalla
739. Script is guión
740. Seat is asiento
741. See is ver
742. Seed is semilla
743. Seek is buscar
744. Seem is parecer
745. Sell is vender
746. Send is enviar
747. Sense is sentido
748. Sensor is sensor
749. Sentence is oración
750. Set is fijar
751. Settings is ajustes

752. Several is varios
753. Shadow is sombra
754. Shake is agitar
755. Shape is figura
756. Share is compartir
757. Shave is afeitar
758. Shelter is refugio
759. Shine is brillar
760. Shoot is disparar
761. Shot is toma
762. Should is deber
763. Show is mostrar
764. Shut is callar
765. Side is lado
766. Sign is firmar
767. Signal is señal
768. Signature is firma
769. Simulate is simular
770. Since is desde
771. Sink is hundirse
772. Sit is sentarse
773. Size is talla
774. Skill is destreza
775. Sky is cielo
776. Sleep is dormir
777. Slide is deslizar
778. Smartphone is teléfono inteligente
779. Smash is aplastar
780. Smell is oler
781. Smoke is fumar
782. Smooth is suave
783. So is entonces
784. Soap is jabón
785. Some is algún
786. Something is algo
787. Sometimes is a veces

788. Song is canción
789. Soon is pronto
790. Sort is tipo
791. Soul is alma
792. Sound is sonido
793. Source is fuente
794. Speak is hablar
795. Speaker is hablante
796. Speech is discurso
797. Speed is velocidad
798. Spell is deletrear
799. Spend is gastar
800. Spin is girar
801. Spoon is cuchara
802. Spread is propagar
803. Spy is espiar
804. Staff is equipo
805. Stage is escenario
806. Stairs is escaleras
807. Stand is levantarse
808. Standard is estándar
809. Stare is mirar fijamente
810. Start is iniciar
811. Statement is declaración
812. Stay is quedarse
813. Steal is robar
814. Step is pisar
815. Stick is adherir
816. Still is todavía
817. Stock is inventario
818. Stop is parar
819. Storage is almacenamiento
820. Story is cuento
821. Streaming is transmisión
822. Strike is huelga
823. Strong is fuerte

824. Study is estudiar
825. Stuff is cosas
826. Style is estilo
827. Subject is sujeto
828. Submit is enviar
829. Substance is sustancia
830. Subtitling is subtitulaje
831. Success is éxito
832. Suddenly is repentinamente
833. Suggest is sugerir
834. Support is apoyar
835. Sure is seguro
836. Surface is superficie
837. Surgery is cirugía
838. Surprise is sorpresa
839. Survey is encuesta
840. Survive is sobrevivir
841. Swear is jurar
842. Swing is balancearse
843. Switch is cambiar
844. Synchronize is sincronizar
845. Syntax is sintaxis
846. Table is mesa
847. Tactic is táctica
848. Take is tomar
849. Talk is hablar
850. Task is tarea
851. Taste is degustar
852. Tax is impuesto
853. Taxi is taxi
854. Teach is enseñar
855. Team is equipo
856. Tear is lágrima
857. Teenager is adolescente
858. Telescope is telescopio
859. Tell is decir

860. Term is término
861. Test is prueba
862. Texture is textura
863. Than is que
864. Thank is agradecer
865. That is eso
866. The is el/la
867. Their is su
868. Theme is tema
869. Then is luego
870. There is ahí
871. These is estos
872. Thick is grueso
873. Thing is cosa
874. Think is pensar
875. Thirst is sed
876. This is esto
877. Those is esos
878. Though is aunque
879. Thought is pensamiento
880. Through is a través
881. Throughout is a lo largo de
882. Throw is tirar
883. Thus is así
884. Ticket is boleto
885. Tide is marea
886. Time is tiempo
887. Tissue is pañuelo
888. Title is título
889. To is para
890. Tobacco is tabaco
891. Today is hoy
892. Together is juntos
893. Tone is tono
894. Tonight is esta noche
895. Too is también

896. Tools is herramientas
897. Top is cima
898. Topic is tema
899. Touch is tocar
900. Toward is hacia
901. Trade is comercio
902. Tragedy is tragedia
903. Training is entrenamiento
904. Transform is transformar
905. Translate is traducir
906. Transport is transporte
907. Trash is basura
908. Travel is viajar
909. Treat is tratar
910. Treatment is tratamiento
911. Tree is árbol
912. Trial is juicio
913. Trip is paseo
914. Trouble is problema
915. Truck is camión
916. Truth is verdad
917. Try is intentar
918. Turn is girar
919. Tutor is tutor
920. Tutorial is tutorial
921. Twin is gemelo
922. Type is teclear
923. Umbrella is paraguas
924. Under is debajo
925. Underline is subrayar
926. Understand is entender
927. Until is hasta
928. Up is arriba
929. Upon is sobre
930. Usually is usualmente
931. Vacillate is vacilar

932. Vast is vasto
933. Vehicle is vehículo
934. Version is versión
935. Very is muy
936. Vibration is vibración
937. Victim is víctima
938. View is vista
939. Viewer is espectador
940. Violation is violación
941. Vocabulary is vocabulario
942. Voice is voz
943. Volcano is volcán
944. Vow is voto
945. Vowel is vocal
946. Wait is esperar
947. Wake is despertar
948. Wall is pared
949. Wander is vagar
950. Want is querer
951. War is guerra
952. Wash is lavar
953. Way is manera
954. Weakness is debilidad
955. Weapon is arma
956. Wear is usar (ropa)
957. Web browser is navegador web
958. Weekend is fin de semana
959. Weight is peso
960. Weird is extraño
961. Welcome is bienvenido
962. Welfare is bienestar
963. Well is bien
964. Wet is mojado
965. What is qué
966. Whatever is como sea
967. When is cuándo

968. Where is dónde
969. Whether is aunque
970. Which is cuál
971. While is mientras
972. Whisper is susurro
973. Whistle is silbido
974. Who is quién
975. Whole is todo
976. Whose is cuyo
977. Why is por qué
978. Wide is amplio
979. Will (do) is haré
980. Win is ganar
981. Window is ventana
982. Wisdom is sabiduría
983. Wise is sabio
984. Wish is deseo
985. With is con
986. Within is dentro
987. Without is sin
988. Wonder is preguntarse
989. Word is palabra
990. Work is trabajar
991. Would is podría
992. Wrap is envolver
993. Wrong is incorrecto
994. Yard is patio
995. Yeah is sí
996. Year is año
997. Yes is sí
998. Yet is aún
999. Your is tu
1000. Youth is juventud

Chapter 14: One Word, Several Meanings.

There are some words in Spanish that may have several meanings. The differentiation depends on the context. Here are some of them:

1. Cuadro can mean Painting or a Geometric figure (Square shaped).

That is a beautiful painting by Picasso
In Spanish this is said:
Ese es un hermoso cuadro de Picasso

My dad has a squared shirt.
In Spanish this is said:
Mi padre tiene una camisa a cuadros.

2. Vino can mean Wine or Third person of the verb "venir" (Come).

He came to my house
In Spanish this is said:
Él vino a mi casa.

She loves wine.
In Spanish this is said:
A ella le encanta el vino.

3. Planta can mean Plant or Synonym of factory.

I have a plant in my living room
In Spanish this is said:
Tengo una planta en mi sala de estar.

He works at a recycling plant.
In Spanish this is said:
Él trabaja en una planta de reciclaje.

4. Banco can mean Bank or Bench

We go to the bank
In Spanish this is said:
Nosotros vamos al banco

She sits on the bench
In Spanish this is said:
Ella se sienta en el banco.

5. Cura can mean Cure or Priest.

They found a cure for varicella
In Spanish this is said:
Ellos encontraron una cura para la varicela.

There is a new priest in our Church.
In Spanish this is said:
Hay un Nuevo cura en nuestra iglesia.

6. Capital can mean Capital of a country or Capital of a company (money)

Canberra is the capital of Australia
In Spanish this is said:
Canberra es la capital de Australia

The company has enough capital for new investments.
In Spanish this is said:
La compañía tiene suficiente capital para nuevas inversiones.

7. Café can mean Coffee or Brown color.

I love coffee
In Spanish this is said:
Me encanta el café

He has brown eyes.
In Spanish this is said:
Él tiene los ojos color café.

8. Chile can mean Country or fruit.

Santiago de Chile is the capital of Chile
In Spanish this is said:
Santiago de Chile es la capital de Chile.

Jalapeños are very spicy chilies.
In Spanish this is said:
Los jalapeños son chiles muy picantes.

9. Cólera can mean Anger or Cholera.

You have to learn to calm your anger.
In Spanish this is said:
Debes aprender a calmar tu cólera.

Cholera is a disease
In Spanish this is said:
El cólera es una enfermedad.

10. Derecho can mean Right or University degree.

Education is a fundamental right.
In Spanish this is said:
La educación es un derecho fundamental.

She studies Law at the university
In Spanish this is said:
Ella estudia Derecho en la Universidad.

11. Destino can mean Destiny or Destination.

We make our own destiny
In Spanish this is said:
Hacemos nuestro propio destino.

Our new destination for this trip is Hawaii
In Spanish this is said:
Nuestro nuevo destino para este viaje es Hawai.

12.   Entrada can mean Entrance or Ticket.

The airport has many entrances.
In Spanish this is said:
El aeropuerto tiene muchas entradas.

I buy the tickets for the concert.
In Spanish this is said:
Yo compro las entradas para el concierto.

13.   Gato can mean Cat or Mechanical Jack.

Sophia has a cat.
In Spanish this is said:
Sophia tiene un gato.

Robert has a new mechanical jack for his car.
In Spanish this is said:
Robert tiene un nuevo gato mecánico para su coche.

14.   Bajo can mean Musical instrument (bass) or Short.

Tim plays the bass
In Spanish this is said:
Tim toca el bajo.

Edgar is very short
In Spanish this is said:
Edgar es muy bajo.

15.   Barra can mean Bar's table or piece of metal.

He likes to drink at the bar of the restaurant
In Spanish this is said:
A él le gusta beber en la barra del restaurante.

They found a metal bar in the backyard.
In Spanish this is said:
Ellos encontraron una barra de metal en el patio.

16. Bota can mean Boots or Third person of the verb "botar" (Throw away).

I have new boots
In Spanish this is said:
Tengo botas nuevas.

She throws away the trash every morning
In Spanish this is said:
Ella bota la basura todas las mañanas.

17. Busto can mean Breast or Bust.

Women have breasts.
In Spanish this is said:
Las mujeres tienen busto.

The museum has a new bust of Napoleon.
In Spanish this is said:
El museo tiene un nuevo busto de Napoleón.

18. Canino can mean Dog or Fangs.

Dogs are canines.
In Spanish this is said:
Los perros son caninos.

The girl lost one of her fangs.
In Spanish this is said:
La niña perdió uno de sus caninos.

19. Carrera can mean Race or Career.

My boyfriend runs in a race.
In Spanish this is said:
Mi novio corre en una carrera.

¿What career do you study?
In Spanish this is said:
¿Qué carrera estudias?

20. Carta can mean Letter or Card.

The soldier writes letters to his family.
In Spanish this is said:
El soldado escribe cartas a su familia.

We like to play cards.
In Spanish this is said:
Nos gusta jugar a las cartas.

21. Clave can mean Key or Password.

Her statement was key to the case.
In Spanish this is said:
Su declaración fue clave para el caso.

You must create a new password.
In Spanish this is said:
Debes crear una nueva clave.

22. Visto can mean Check mark or Seen.

Right answers get a checkmark.
In Spanish this is said:
Las respuestas correctas obtienen un visto.

I have already seen this movie.
In Spanish this is said:
Ya he visto esta película.

23. Arco can mean Bow or Arch.

You need a bow to throw the arrow.
In Spanish this is said:
Necesitas un arco para lanzar la fleche.

The Arch of Triumph is in Paris.
In Spanish this is said:
El Arco del Triunfo está en París.

24.   Blanco can mean White or Target.

His favourite colour is white.
In Spanish this is said:
Su color favorito es el blanco.

They aim at the target.
In Spanish this is said:
Ellos apuntan al blanco.

25.   Libra can mean British pound or Zodiac's sign.

That cost 35 pounds.
In Spanish this is said:
Eso cuesta 35 libras.

Their zodiac sign is Libra.
In Spanish this is said:
Su signo zodiacal es Libra.

26.   Corredor can mean Corridor or Runner.

The corridor is very long.
In Spanish this is said:
El corredor es muy largo.

Africans are excellent runners.
In Spanish this is said:
Los africanos son corredores excelentes.

27.   Goma can mean Bubble gum or Eraser.

Some lollipops have bubble gum inside
In Spanish this is said:
Algunos chupetes tienen goma de mascar adentro.

May I borrow your eraser?
In Spanish this is said:
¿Me prestas tu goma de borrar?

28.   Mango can mean Fruit or Handle.

My favourite fruit is mango.
In Spanish this is said:
Mi fruta favorita es el mango.

The teacup has a broken handle
In Spanish this is said:
La taza de té tiene el mango roto.

29.   Pico can mean Peak or Beak.

He likes to climb snowy peaks.
In Spanish this is said:
A él le gusta escalar picos nevados.

That bird has a broken beak.
In Spanish this is said:
Esa ave tiene el pico roto.

30.   Pie can mean Unit of length (feet)/ Part of the human body.

That has 20 feets long.
In Spanish this is said:
Eso tiene 20 pies de largo.

I have small feet.
In Spanish this is said:
Tengo pies pequeños.

31. Placa can mean Badge, Plate or Vehicle number plate.

Police officers have a badge.
In Spanish this is said:
Los oficiales de policías tienen una placa.

Tectonics plates are always moving.
In Spanish this is said:
Las placas tectónicas siempre se mueven.

What's your vehicle's number plate?
In Spanish this is said:
¿Cuál es el número de placa de tu vehículo?

32. Tienda can mean Store or Tent.

I like the new store.
In Spanish this is said:
Me gusta la nueva tienda.

We need a tent to go camping.
In Spanish this is said:
Necesitamos una tienda para ir a acampar.

33. Regla can mean Ruler, Rules or Menstruation.

May I borrow your ruler?
In Spanish this is said:
¿Me prestas tu regla?

You have to respect de rules of the game.
In Spanish this is said:
Debes respetar las reglas del juego.

Menstruation changes women's mood.
In Spanish this is said:
La regla cambia el estado de ánimo de las mujeres.

34. Ratón can mean Mouse (Animal) or A Computer Mouse

Mickey is a mouse.
In Spanish this is said:
Mickey es un ratón.

My computer's mouse is blue.
In Spanish this is said:
El ratón de mi computadora es azul.

35. Timbre can mean Doorbell or Stamp.

Ring the doorbell, please.
In Spanish this is said:
Toca el timbre, por favor.

You need another stamp for this document.
In Spanish this is said:
Necesitas otro timbre para este documento.

36. Portero can mean Doorman or Goalkeeper.

Rick is the new doorman.
In Spanish this is said:
Rick es el nuevo portero.

The goalkeeper protects the football goal.
In Spanish this is said:
El portero protege la portería.

37. Palo can mean Stick or Cards Suit.

Throw the stick and the dog will bring it back
In Spanish this is said:
Lanza el palo y el perro lo traerá de vuelta.

All my cards are of the same suit.
In Spanish this is said:
Todas mis cartas son del mismo palo.

38. Masa can mean Dough, Pastry or Mass.

Donnuts dough should be smooth.
In Spanish this is said:
La masa de los donuts debe ser suave.

I prepared the pastry for the pie.
In Spanish this is said:
Preparé la masa para el pastel.

There is a big mass of people there.
In Spanish this is said:
Hay una gran masa de gente ahí.

39. Llave can mean Key, Spanner or Grappling.

He always loses his keys.
In Spanish this is said:
Él siempre pierde sus llaves.

He fixes the machine with a spanner.
In Spanish this is said:
Él repara la máquina con una llave.

In the martial arts, they use many grappling.
In Spanish this is said:
En las artes marciales, se usan muchas llaves.

40. Juego can mean Game or First person of the verb "jugar" (play).

I love this game.
In Spanish this is said:
Me encanta este juego.

I play volleyball with my friends
In Spanish this is said:
Yo juego vóleibol con mis amigos.

41. Sumo can mean Sport (Sumo) or First person of the verb "sumar" (Sum)

He practices sumo.
In Spanish this is said:
Él practica sumo.

I add with the calculator.
In Spanish this is said:
Yo sumo con la calculadora.

42. Yema can mean Fingertips or Yolk.

The egg has yolk and white.
In Spanish this is said:
El huevo tiene yema y clara.

In volleyball, you hit the ball with your fingertips.
In Spanish this is said:
En vóleibol se golpea la pelota con la yema de los dedos.

43. Villano can mean Villain or Peasants.

He is the villain of the story.
In Spanish this is said:
Él es el villano de la película.

They are peasants from the village.
In Spanish this is said:
Ellos son villanos de la villa.

44. Vencer can mean Defeat or Expire.

He has to defeat the other fighter.
In Spanish this is said:
Él debe vencer al otro luchador.

The milk expires tomorrow.
In Spanish this is said:
La leche vence mañana.

45.   Traje can mean Suit or First person past tense of the verb "Traer" (Bring).

Logan's suit is grey.
In Spanish this is said:
El traje de Logan es gris.

I brought a big soda for the party.
In Spanish this is said:
Yo traje una gaseosa grande para la fiesta.

46.   Tipo can mean Type or Guy.

He is not my type of man.
In Spanish this is said:
Él no es mi tipo de hombre.

A guy was following me.
In Spanish this is said:
Un tipo me estaba siguiendo.

47.   Tarde can mean Late or Afternoon.

It is too late.
In Spanish this is said:
Es muy tarde.

Good afternoon!
In Spanish this is said:
¡Buenas tardes!

48.   Sol can mean Sun or Music note (G)

The sun is yellow.
In Spanish this is said:
El sol es amarillo.

G is a musical note.
In Spanish this is said:
Sol es una nota musical.

49.   Soplo can mean Blow or Heart murmur.

I blow the candles and make a wish.
In Spanish this is said:
Soplo las velas y pido un deseo.

My grandpa has a heart murmur.
In Spanish this is said:
Mi abuelo tiene un soplo en el corazón.

50.   Sierra can mean Saw or Mountain Range.

He uses a saw.
In Spanish this is said:
Él usa una sierra.

Spain's mountain ranges are beautiful.
In Spanish this is said:
Las sierras de España son hermosas.

51.   Salsa can mean Sauce or Salsa (Dance).

I prepare a delicious hot sauce.
In Spanish this is said:
Yo preparo una deliciosa salsa picante.

She dances salsa.
In Spanish this is said:
Ella baila salsa.

52. Rosa can mean Rose or Pink.

Roses are red.
In Spanish this is said:
Las rosas son rojas.

She has pink hair.
In Spanish this is said:
Ella tiene el cabello rosa.

53. Real can mean Real or Royal.

The movie is based on a real story.
In Spanish this is said:
La película está basada en una historia real.

They are the royal family.
In Spanish this is said:
Ellos son la familia Real.

54. Pluma can mean Feather or Pen.

The swan's feathers are white.
In Spanish this is said:
Las plumas del cisne son blancas.

I need a pen to sign.
In Spanish this is said:
Necesito una pluma para firmar.

55. Pila can mean Battery or Pile.

The toy needs batteries.
In Spanish this is said:
El juguete necesita pilas.

That is a big pile of books.
In Spanish this is said:
Esa es una gran pila de libros.

56. Heroína can mean Drug (Heroin) or Heroine.

The heroin is a drug.
In Spanish this is said:
La heroína es una droga.

There are heroes and heroines.
In Spanish this is said:
Hay héroes y heroínas.

57. Este can mean East or This.

The sun rises in the east.
In Spanish this is said:
El sol sale por el este.

This is my book.
In Spanish this is said:
Este es mi libro.

58. Don can mean Gift or Mr.

She has a special gift.
In Spanish this is said:
Ella tiene un don especial.

Mr. Thomas is my neighbor.
In Spanish this is said:
Don Thomas es mi vecino.

59. Bolsa can mean Bag or Stock Exchange.

Could you help me with the bags?
In Spanish this is said:
¿Puedes ayudarme con las bolsas?

The stock exchange of New York.
In Spanish this is said:
La bolsa de Nueva York.

60. Bomba can mean Bomb or Pump.

The bomb explotes.
In Spanish this is said:
La bomba explota.

The water tank has a new pump.
In Spanish this is said:
El tanque de agua tiene una bomba nueva.

61. Vela can mean Candle or Sail.

Turn off the candle.
In Spanish this is said:
Apaga la vela.

Raise the sails!
In Spanish this is said:
¡Eleven las velas!

62. Estado can mean State, Government or State (physical presence).

Every state has a capital.
In Spanish this is said:
Cada estado tiene una capital.

That is responsibility of the State.
In Spanish this is said:
Eso es responsabilidad del Estado.

He is in a critical state.
In Spanish this is said:
Está en un estado crítico.

63. Genio can mean Genius, Genie or Temper.

You are a genius.
In Spanish this is said:
Eres un genio.

The magic lamp has a genie inside.
In Spanish this is said:
La lámpara mágica tiene un genio adentro.

He has a bad temper.
In Spanish this is said:
Él tiene un mal genio.

64. Granada can mean Pomegranate or Grenade.

The pomegranate is a fruit.
In Spanish this is said:
La granada es una fruta.

The grenade did not explode.
In Spanish this is said:
La granada no explotó.

65. Gancho can mean Hanger or Hook.

I hang my dress on a hanger.
In Spanish this is said:
Yo cuelgo mi vestido en un gancho.

He knocked him out with a left hook.
In Spanish this is said:
Él lo noqueó con un gancho izquierdo.

66. Hoja can mean Sheet, Leaves or Blade.

I need a sheet for the exam.
In Spanish this is said:
Necesito una hoja para el examen.

Trees have leaves.
In Spanish this is said:
Los árboles tienen hojas.

The sword blade is blunt.
In Spanish this is said:
La hoja de la espada está desafilada.

67. Lima can mean Lime or Nail file.

I like lime juice.
In Spanish this is said:
Me gusta el jugo de lima.

I use a nail file for my nails.
In Spanish this is said:
Uso una lima para mis uñas.

68. Lista can mean List or Smart.

He has a to-do list.
In Spanish this is said:
Él tiene una lista de cosas por hacer.

She is very smart.
In Spanish this is said:
Ella es muy lista.

69. Llama can mean Flame, to call or Llama (Animal).

The fire flames grow.
In Spanish this is said:
Las llamas del incendio crecen.

Call you father, please!
In Spanish this is said:
Llama a tu padre, por favor.

Llamas are animals.
In Spanish this is said:
Las llamas son animales.

70.   Manzana can mean Apple or Block.

Apples are red or green.
In Spanish this is said:
Las manzanas son rojas o verdes.

They live three blocks from here.
In Spanish this is said:
Ellos viven a tres manzanas de aquí.

71.   Metro can mean Subway or Meter.

The subway station is underground.
In Spanish this is said:
La estación del metro es subterránea.

This has one meter and a half.
In Spanish this is said:
Esto mide un metro y medio.

72.   Damas can mean Plural of "Lady" or Checkers.

That is the ladies' bathroom.
In Spanish this is said:
Ese es el baño de damas.

My grandpa plays checkers very good.
In Spanish this is said:
Mi abuelo juega a las damas muy bien.

73.   Casco can mean Helmet or Hull.

Don't forget to wear the helmet.
In Spanish this is said:
No olvides usar el casco.

The ship's hull is rusted.
In Spanish this is said:
El casco del barco está oxidado.

74.   Yunque: can mean Anvil or Bone of the ear (Incus).

Blacksmiths use anvils.
In Spanish this is said:
Los herreros usan yunques.

The incus is a bone of the ear.
In Spanish this is said:
El yunque es un hueso de la oreja.

75.   Tubo can mean Tube or Past tense of the verb "tener" (have).

The tube is broken.
In Spanish this is said:
El tubo está roto.

She had a pet.
In Spanish this is said:
Ella tubo una mascota.

76.   Orden can mean Command, Order or Warrant.

It's not a favour, it's a command.
In Spanish this is said:
No es un favour, es una orden.

You need to have order in you room.
In Spanish this is said:
Necesitas tener orden en tu habitación.

The officers need a warrant to search the house.
In Spanish this is said:
Los oficiales necesitan una orden para reviser la casa.

77.   Nada can mean Nothing or Third person of the verb "nadar" (Swim).

Nothing happens.
In Spanish this is said:
No pasa nada.

The girl swims very good.
In Spanish this is said:
La niña nada muy bien.

78.   Muñeca can mean Doll or Wrist.

The girl has many dolls.
In Spanish this is said:
La niña tiene muchas muñecas.

My wrist hurts.
In Spanish this is said:
Me duele la muñeca.

79.   Juicio can mean Wisdom, Judgement or Trial.

His mind does not have a bit of wisdom.
In Spanish this is said:
Su mente no tiene un poquito de juicio.

You cannot make a judgement without knowing the context.
In Spanish this is said:
No puedes hacer un juicio sin saber el contexto.

The prisoner goes to a trial.
In Spanish this is said:
El prisionero va a un juicio.

80. Fondo can mean Fund, Bottom or Background.

The foundation raises funds for those in need.
In Spanish this is said:
La fundación recolecta fondos para los necesitados.

He gets to the bottom of the pool.
In Spanish this is said:
Él llega hasta el fondo de la piscina.

I want to know the background of the problem.
In Spanish this is said:
Quiero saber el fondo del problema.

81. Estación can mean Station or Season.

The bus station is near my house.
In Spanish this is said:
La estación de buses está cerca de mi casa.

My favorite season of the year is summer.
In Spanish this is said:
Mi estación favorita del año es el verano.

82. Corte can mean Cut or Court.

He has a new haircut.
In Spanish this is said:
Él tiene un nuevo corte de cabello.

The court has a new judge.
In Spanish this is said:
La corte tiene un nuevo juez.

83. Cola can mean Glue, Soda, or Tail.

The glue is white.
In Spanish this is said:
La cola es blanca.

I want a soda.
In Spanish this is said:
Quiero una cola.

The cat has a long tail.
In Spanish this is said:
El gato tiene una cola larga.

84.   Capa can mean Cloak, Cape or Layer.

The owner of the circus wears a cloak.
In Spanish this is said:
El dueño del circo usa una capa.

Some superheroes wear capes.
In Spanish this is said:
Algunos súper héroes usan capas.

The cake has several layers.
In Spanish this is said:
El pastel tiene varias capas.

85.   Columna can mean Backbone or Column.

He has a pain in his backbone.
In Spanish this is said:
Él tiene un dolor en la columna.

The church has eight columns.
In Spanish this is said:
La iglesia tiene seis columnas.

86.   Globo can mean Balloon or Globe.

Kids love balloons.
In Spanish this is said:
Los niños aman los globos.

The globe has two poles.
In Spanish this is said:
El globo terráqueo tiene dos polos.

87. Corriente can mean Current or Power.

The river has a strong current of water.
In Spanish this is said:
El río tiene una fuerte corriente de agua.

There is no electric power here.
In Spanish this is said:
No hay corriente eléctrica aquí.

88. Dado can mean Given or Dice.

You have given a lot.
In Spanish this is said:
Tú has dado mucho.

Throw the dice.
In Spanish this is said:
Lanza el dado.

89. Frente can mean Forehead or Front.

He has a big forehead.
In Spanish this is said:
Él tiene la frente grande.

The army has a front.
In Spanish this is said:
El ejército tiene un frente.

90. Radio can mean Radio, Radius or Radium.

I listen to the radio.
In Spanish this is said:
Yo escucho la radio.

The radius of the circle.
In Spanish this is said:
El radio del círculo.

Radium is a chemical element.
In Spanish this is said:
El radio es un elemento químico.

91.   Cubo can mean Cube or Bucket.

The cube is a geometric figure.
In Spanish this is said:
El cubo es una figura geométrica.

I need a bucket of water.
In Spanish this is said:
Necesito un cubo de agua.

92.   Bien can mean Alright or Good (possesion).

We are alright.
In Spanish this is said:
Nosotros estamos bien.

They divide their goods.
In Spanish this is said:
Ellos dividen los bienes.

93.   Cámara can mean Camera or Chamber.

The photographer uses a camera.
In Spanish this is said:
El fotógrafo usa una cámara.

The castle has a secret chamber.
In Spanish this is said:
El castillo tiene una cámara secreta.

94. Cuarto can mean Quarter, Room or Fourth.

It's a quarter past eight.
In Spanish this is said:
Son las ocho y cuarto.

The boy's room is green.
In Spanish this is said:
El cuarto del niño es verde.

He is in fourth grade.
In Spanish this is said:
Él está en cuarto grado.

95. Escudo can mean Shield or Emblem.

Vikings use shields.
In Spanish this is said:
Los vikingos usan escudos.

That is our family's emblem.
In Spanish this is said:
Ese es el escudo de nuestra familia.

96. Física can mean Physics or Physicist.

They have physics class.
In Spanish this is said:
Ellos tienen clase de física.

She is a physicist.
In Spanish this is said:
Ella es una física.

97. Meta can mean Goal or Finish.

We all have goals for the new year.
In Spanish this is said:
Todos tenemos metas para el nuevo año.

The runner crosses the finish line.
In Spanish this is said:
El corredor cruza la meta.

98.   Partir can mean Leave or Break.

The airplane leaves in five minutes.
In Spanish this is said:
El avión parte en cinco minutos.

The cup broke.
In Spanish this is said:
La taza se partió.

99.   Periódico can mean Newspaper or Periodic.

My dad reads the newspaper.
In Spanish this is said:
Mi papá lee el periódico.

The climate has periodic variations.
In Spanish this is said:
El clima tiene variaciones periódicas.

100.   Plancha can mean Iron or Grill.

Iron your clothes.
In Spanish this is said:
Plancha tu ropa.

She likes to cook on the grill.
In Spanish this is said:
A ella le gusta cocinar a la plancha.

Chapter 15: Small Real Life Stories

1. I went to the shops today, then I went to the beach and had a burger, it was a fun day.
In Spanish this is said:
Hoy fui de compras, luego fui a la playa y comí una hamburguesa, fue un día divertido.

2. This weekend I went to a party with a lot of people. The music was great and the food was delicious.
In Spanish this is said:
El fin de semana fui a una fiesta con mucha gente. La música era genial y la comida estaba deliciosa.

3. Yesterday, my friend was late to school because she forgot her book at home.
In Spanish this is said:
Ayer, mi amiga llegó tarde a la escuela porque olvidó su libro en casa.

4. My brother loves his wife and I think their relationship will last forever.
In Spanish this is said:
Mi hermano ama a su esposa y yo creo que su relación durará para siempre.

5. The videogames competition ended early. The red team won without any problem.
In Spanish this is said:
La competencia de videojuegos terminó temprano. El equipo rojo ganó sin problemas.

6. I saw several photos of my college friends in our last trip together.
In Spanish this is said:
Vi varias fotos de mis amigos de la universidad, en nuestro último viaje juntos.

7. Jaime felt during the baseball game, and now he is at the hospital because he broke his arm.
In Spanish this is said:
Jaime se cayó en el juego de béisbol y ahora está en el hospital porque se rompió el brazo.

8. I like to buy tomatoes outside the city because they are fresh and economic.
In Spanish this is said:
Me gusta comprar tomates fuera de la ciudad porque son frescos y económicos.

9. I have a new boss, and he is better than the former one.
In Spanish this is said:
Tengo un nuevo jefe y es mejor que el anterior.

10. I like to travel and visit different countries with my family.
In Spanish this is said:
Me gusta viajar y visitar diferentes países con mi familia.

11. I love animals, I have one cat, two dogs, and three horses. Our house is very big.
In Spanish this is said:
Me encantan los animales, tengo un gato, dos perros y tres caballos. Nuestra casa es muy grande.

12. I have a big group of friends. We are all different, we have different ages, ideas, and opinions, but I love each one of them.
In Spanish this is said:
Tengo un grupo grande de amigos. Todos somos diferentes, tenemos diferentes edades, ideas y opiniones, pero amo a cada uno de ellos.

13. She never drove a car before, until she met her new friend.

In Spanish this is said:
Ella nunca antes condujo un coche, hasta que conoció a su nueva amiga.

14. That guy works a lot to develop his research.
In Spanish this is said:
Ese chico trabaja mucho para desarrollar su investigación.

15. I like to spend my money on the local market. They sell great things.
In Spanish this is said:
Me gusta gastar mi dinero en el mercado local. Venden cosas geniales.

16. My mother always says: Read a book, be a good person and live.
In Spanish this is said:
Mi madre siempre dice: Lee un libro, sé buena persona y vive.

17. That girl likes to read history books.
In Spanish this is said:
A esa niña le gusta leer libros de historia.

18. My father walks early in the morning before going to work.
In Spanish this is said:
Mi padre camina temprano en las mañanas antes de ir a trabajar.

19. My mother said: If you don't clean your room, you cannot go to the movies.
In Spanish this is said:
Mi madre dijo: Si no limpias tu habitación, no puedes ir al cine.

20. He likes to walk along the road, from his house to his mother's house.

In Spanish this is said:
A él le gusta caminar a lo largo de la vía de su casa a la casa de su madre.

21. Smartphones are the new technology of this generation. Every day, there are new model, new apps, and new features. But they also get more expensive
In Spanish this is said:
Los teléfonos inteligentes son la nueva tecnología de esta generación. Todos los días hay nuevos modelos, nuevas aplicaciones y nuevas características. Aunque también son más costosos

22. The process of learning does not depend on the size of your brain, it depends on your interest, enthusiasm and motivation.
In Spanish this is said:
El proceso de aprender no depende del tamaño de tu cerebro, depende de tu interés, entusiasmo y dedicación.

23. Lucas types very fast on his computer, sometimes you cannot see the keyboard, you just see his hands moving.
In Spanish this is said:
Lucas escribe muy rápido en su computadora, a veces no se puede ver el teclado, solamente ves sus manos moverse.

24. I went to a zoo in Brazil last year. There are a lot of animals there, it is a huge place.
In Spanish this is said:
El año pasado fui a un zoológico en Brasil. Hay muchos animales allá, es un lugar enorme.

25. Daniel loves to travel. He knows almost every country in the world. His favourites are Australia, Venezuela, Ireland and Switzerland.
In Spanish this is said:
Daniel ama viajar. Él conoce casi todos los países del mundo, sus favoritos son Australia, Venezuela, Irlanda y Suiza.

26. Juliet loves to cook and create new dishes. Sometimes she shares her recipes, and uses odd names for each one.
In Spanish this is said:
Julieta ama cocinar y crear nuevos platos. A veces comparte sus recetas y usa nombres raros para cada una.

27. Ian and Liam are twins, but Ian is tall and has blue eyes, but Liam is small and has green eyes.
In Spanish this is said:
Ian y Liam son gemelos, pero Ian es alto y tiene los ojos azules y Liam es pequeño y tiene los ojos verdes.

28. I love to dance and my sister loves to sing. We are the perfect team for parties
In Spanish this is said:
Me encanta bailar y a mi hermana le encanta cantar. Somos el equipo perfecto para las fiestas.

29. Jordan has three classes on Mondays: Math, Science and Psychology. Those classes are difficult, but he still likes them.
In Spanish this is said:
Jordan tiene tres clases los lunes: matemáticas, ciencias y psicología. Esas clases son difíciles, pero a Jordan le gustan.

30. David drives a big truck to work in the farm, and he carries a lot of animals, like cows, roosters, pigs, and ducks. He likes to imitate their sounds when he drives.
In Spanish this is said:
David maneja un gran camión para trabajar en la granja, y transporta muchos animales como vacas, gallos, cerdos y patos. A David le gusta imitar sus sonidos cuando conduce.

31. Matt studies French, but he has troubles to conjugate verbs. So, he invented a way to practice with cards and a board.
In Spanish this is said:

Matt estudia francés, pero tiene problemas para conjugar los verbos. Entonces, inventó una manera de practicar con cartas y una pizarra.

32. My computer's battery is broken, so I have to connect the charger to use it. Sometimes, I forget the charger when I go to school and that is very frustrating.
In Spanish this is said:
La batería de mi computadora está dañada, entonces debo conectar el cargador para usarla. A veces, olvido el cargador cuando voy a la escuela y eso es muy frustrante.

33. Grandparents are not good with technology, but they are excellent at telling stories and cooking delicious food.
In Spanish this is said:
Los abuelos no son buenos con la tecnología, pero son excelentes contando cuentos y cocinando comida deliciosa.

34. I do not like horror movies. I always scream when the ghost appears.
In Spanish this is said:
No me gustan las películas de horror. Siempre grito cuando aparece el fantasma.

35. My Dad's office is far from the city. Every day, he goes out early to avoid traffic
In Spanish this is said:
La oficina de mi papá es lejos de la ciudad. Todos los días, sale temprano para evitar el tráfico.

36. George travels almost every year. He selects a country or a city from the map, saves money, makes reservations and makes an itinerary.
In Spanish this is said:
George viaja casi todos los años. Él selecciona un país o una ciudad en el mapa, guarda dinero, hace reservas y hace un itinerario.

37. Cognates are words that helps to learn a new language. If you remember all of them, you improve your vocabulary.
In Spanish this is said:
Los cognados son palabras que ayudan a aprender un nuevo idioma. Si los recuerdas todos, mejoras tu vocabulario.

38. When you go to the airport, write all the words you see on the walls, the exits and everywhere. Then, look for them in other languages. In that way, you won't be lost at any airport around the world.
In Spanish this is said:
Cuando vayas al aeropuerto, escribe todas las palabras que veas en las paredes, las salidas y en todas partes. Luego, búscalas en otros idiomas, de esa manera, no te perderás en ningún aeropuerto del mundo.

39. Sometimes, writing an essay is difficult. All you have to do is write every idea that comes to your mind, then try to organize them. It helps to define your topic for the essay.
In Spanish this is said:
A veces, escribir un ensayo es difícil. Todo lo que debes hacer es escribir cada idea que venga a tu mente, luego trata de ordenarlas. Eso ayuda a definir el tema de tu ensayo.

40. Journalists have to know grammar, because they write a lot and they must do it correctly.
In Spanish this is said:
Los periodistas deben saber de gramática, porque ellos escriben mucho y deben hacerlo correctamente.

41. Mary has four jobs. She is a secretary, a nurse, a mechanic, and a makeup artist. She is always busy.
In Spanish this is said:
Mary tiene cuatro trabajos. Ella es secretaria, enfermera, mecánica y maquilladora. Siempre está ocupada.

42. Jamie is sad, he washed his car yesterday and today is a rainy day. His car is dirty again.
In Spanish this is said:
Jamie está triste, él lavó su coche ayer y hoy es un día lluvioso. Su coche está sucio otra vez.

43. Kids have fun in the park every weekend. They run, jump and play.
In Spanish this is said:
Los niños se divierten en el parque cada fines de semana. Ellos corren, saltan y juegan.

44. Romantic movies always have a scene with a sunset or a sunrise. It's classic.
In Spanish this is said:
Las películas románticas siempre tienen una escena con un atardecer o un amanecer, es clásico.

45. France has many castles. They have different sizes, big, medium, small or huge.
In Spanish this is said:
Francia tiene muchos castillos. Tiene diferentes tamaños, grandes, medianos, pequeños o enormes.

46. The queen of England has white, curly hair and blue eyes. She is a very elegant woman.
In Spanish this is said:
La reina de Inglaterra tiene el cabello blanco, rizado y los ojos azules. Ella es una mujer muy elegante.

47. I have a big family. We all live far away, but we have especial occasions when we all meet at our grandparent's house. Those are great meetings.
In Spanish this is said:
Tengo una familia grande. Todos vivimos muy lejos, pero tenemos ocasiones especiales en las que nos reunimos en casa de mis abuelos. Esas son reuniones geniales.

48. There are many buildings in my city. All of them are very tall and have big elevators. I prefer to use the stairs because is good for my health.
In Spanish this is said:
Hay muchos edificios en mi ciudad. Todos son muy altos y tienen ascensores grandes. Yo prefiero usar las escaleras porque es bueno para mi salud.

49. Kids must know that they cannot eat without washing their hands. Adults have to wash their hands too.
In Spanish this is said:
Los niños deben saber que no pueden comer sin lavarse las manos. Los adultos también deben lavarse las manos.

50. My dog loves me, and he wakes me up every morning with a kiss. Sometimes he bites my nose. That make me laugh.
In Spanish this is said:
Mi perro me ama y me despierta todas las mañanas con un beso. A veces muerde mi nariz. Eso me hace reír.

51. I drink coffee every afternoon at 4pm with my mom at a small cafe. That appointment is always in my schedule.
In Spanish this is said:
Yo bebo café todas las tardes a las 4pm con mi mamá en una pequeña cafetería. Esa cita siempre está en mi horario.

52. Bodyguards must be strong, brave men. They protect famous people from paparazzi, fanatics, and every sort of danger.
In Spanish this is said:
Los guardaespaldas deben ser hombres fuertes y valientes. Ellos protegen a los famosos de los paparazzi, fanáticos y todo tipo de peligro.

53. Karen is a doctor, she knows every organ, muscle, part and bone of the body. She is very good helping people. She never gets sick; she is very healthy.

In Spanish this is said:
Karen es doctora, ella conoce cada órgano, músculo, parte y hueso del cuerpo. Ella es muy buena ayudando a las personas. Ella nunca se enferma, es muy saludable.

54. Chris is a very odd man. He is always in a bad mood, he is always angry and nobody know why.
In Spanish this is said:
Chris es un hombre muy extraño. Siempre está de mal humor, siempre está enojado y nadie sabe por qué.

55. Kids are funny. They ask many things, sometimes the same things, and even if you answer already, they will keep asking.
In Spanish this is said:
Los niños son graciosos. Ellos preguntas muchas cosas, a veces las mismas cosas, incluso si ya respondiste, seguirán preguntando.

56. Laura draws beautiful figures. She is very creative. Her art is abstract but very interesting.
In Spanish this is said:
Laura dibuja hermosas figuras. Ella es muy creativa, su arte es abstracta pero muy interesante.

57. Robert is a fashion designer. He designs dresses and his wife wears them. She is a model
In Spanish this is said:
Robert es un diseñador de moda. Él diseña vestidos y su esposa los usa. Ella es modelo.

58. Green represents nature. Red represents love. Blue represents the sky and white represents peace.
In Spanish this is said:
El verde representa la naturaleza. El rojo representa el amor. El azul representa el cielo y el blanco representa la paz.

59. Elena is my neighbour, she is from Russia and she decorates her house with Russian dolls.
In Spanish this is said:
Elena es mi vecina, ella es de Rusia y decora su casa con muñecas rusas.

60. If you look at the time when you are working, time will pass slow. If you forget about time, it will pass faster.
In Spanish this is said:
Si miras la hora cuando está trabajando, el tiempo pasará lento. Si te olvidas del tiempo, las horas pasaran más rápido.

61. My university has a sports competition, where the winner team receive an award and a free trip to any place they want to visit.
In Spanish this is said:
Mi Universidad tiene una competencia deportiva, donde el equipo ganador recibe un premio y un viaje gratis a cualquier lugar que quieran visitar.

62. My house is between two malls. So, I have a lot of places to shop.
In Spanish this is said:
Mi casa está entre dos centros comerciales. Entonces, tengo muchos lugares para ir de compras.

63. My favorite things to do on weekends are: Watch movies, read a book, play the piano, and rest.
In Spanish this is said:
Mis cosas favoritas para hacer los fines de semana son: Ver películas, leer un libro, tocar el piano y descansar.

64. My cousin participates at the Olympics games. He is a gymnast.
In Spanish this is said:
Mi primo participa en los juegos olímpicos. Él es gimnasta.

65. Telling the truth is one of the most important things in life.
In Spanish this is said:
Decir la verdad es una de las cosas más importantes en la vida.

66. My grandma said: Share, enjoy and laugh. That is the secret of life.
In Spanish this is said:
Mi abuela decía: Comparte, disfruta y ríe, ese es el secreto de la vida.

67. The reason why sometimes we disagree with some people is simply because we have different perspectives.
In Spanish this is said:
La razón por la que a veces no estamos de acuerdo con algunas personas, es simplemente porque tenemos diferentes perspectivas.

68. Do not compare yourself with others. We are all different, we are all unique, no one is better than anyone, and we are perfect in our own way.
In Spanish this is said:
No te compares con otros. Todos somos diferentes, todos somos únicos, nadie es mejor que nadie y todos somos perfectos a nuestra propia manera.

69. She does not know how to swim because she is afraid to drown. Fear is a strong emotion; she has to learn to overcome fear.
In Spanish this is said:
Ella no sabe nadar porque tiene miedo de ahogarse. El miedo es una emoción fuerte, debe aprender a superar el miedo.

70. Breath, everything is going to be ok.
In Spanish this is said:
Respira, todo va a estar bien.

Conclusion

If you got this far, you have done an amazing job. You proved to yourself that enthusiasm and interest is all you need to learn a language. Surely, you realized that you already knew some words, thanks to cognates. Now, you understand sentences, and have trained your ear to some sounds you are not used to. If you think you need to improve some things, do it! Go back to the previous chapters and repeat them as much as you need. Remember, this is not a race or a competition, it is a process. Thanks to the Chapter 14 you can understand why sometimes you did not understand some phrases in Spanish, maybe it was because you only knew one meaning of that certain word. The Small Real Life Stories are also good for training your ear to Spanish pronunciation, as well as to understand the structure of Spanish sentences.

The vocabulary you have now is enough for you to have a strong base. That means, you are able to understand daily situations and you can transmit a message with full meaning. You can travel and understand basic conversations, or know where you are by reading the signs. You can practice anytime and anywhere, how? Easy, try to name all the things around you in Spanish or just simply plug in your earphoens and listen to this audiobook. In that way, you can practice memory, vocabulary and pronunciation whenever. Another exercise is for you to write in Spanish. You can also send a text to some friends in Spanish. Do the best you can with what you have. As mentioned before, you can find your own method to learn, and now to practice. From now on, it's up to you to continue your process of learning. The Spanish language does not end here; this is just the beginning.

www.ingramcontent.com/pod-product-compliance
Lightning Source LLC
Chambersburg PA
CBHW072055290426
44110CB00014B/1697